MOVING TO ATLANTA

THE UN-TOURIST GUIDE

ANNE WAINSCOTT-SARGENT

ISBN 978-0-9966079-9-5 (soft cover)

ISBN 978-0-9972461-0-0 (e-book)

To Jeff, with love—what fun we've had rediscovering why Atlanta, more than ever, is our chosen city.

CONTENTS

FOREWORD

I'll never forget the first time I really visited Atlanta—other than passing through it on I-75 on the way to Florida from my native Ohio. It was July 1996, and I was here from AT&T's headquarters in New Jersey to "cover" the Olympic Games for AT&T's employee magazine.

I recall standing on Centennial Olympic Park's main stage with a corporate photographer as the Gambler himself, Kenny Rogers, crooned "Through the Years," and later, walking through the park at twilight as kids splashed around in the Fountain of Rings. A pair of Japanese radio journalists interviewed me outside the iconic Fox Theatre after watching "Gone with the Wind," the Civil War epic penned by Margaret Mitchell.

After these memorable moments and experiencing the hospitality of Atlantans from all walks of life, Georgia was most definitely on my mind. When I got the chance to move here two years later, I didn't hesitate. Atlanta was my fresh start: it's where I met my husband, started a business, and had a family—it's where I built a life. And, except for a brief sojourn to South Florida, it's where I've stayed.

Why do I love Atlanta? It's a combination of things—the people, the creative and entrepreneurial spirit that thrives here, the lush beauty, and the history, too. Atlanta is a chosen city, as another northern transplant, Dante Stephensen, said while sharing with me his own reasons for making Atlanta his home nearly five decades ago.

I hope reading *Moving to Atlanta: The Un-Tourist Guide* will help you discover for yourself if this city of neighborhoods is your chosen city.

#1. Amazing Weather

A temperate climate with mild winters and extended spring and fall seasons means that residents can be outside year-round. Because Atlanta is 1,000 feet above sea level, it cools off in the evenings, even in the summer.

#2. Plentiful Jobs

The Metro Atlanta region was No. 2 in the nation for job growth (up 3.2 percent), and No. 4 for total jobs added (79,600), according to survey data from the Atlanta Regional Commission. The fastest-growing employment sectors are leisure and hospitality, construction and professional and business services.

#3. Affordable Cost of Living

A lower cost of living in Atlanta for major expenses like housing, clothing, food, and gasoline help keep the region's cost of living below the U.S. average—and well below those of most major metropolitan areas. The median sale price for an Atlanta home is currently $177,500.

#4. Bustling Economy

With Georgia Tech leading the charge with its Technology Square innovation district in the heart of Midtown, Fortune 500 firms like NCR Corporation are moving their headquarters to the city to tap into Atlanta's talent pool. For three years' running, Georgia has been named the best state in the nation for business. So many Fortune 1000 firms are moving here that two-term Atlanta Mayor Kasim Reed has called Atlanta the "New Headquarters Capital."

#5. Affordable and Convenient Travel

Hartsfield-Jackson Atlanta International Airport is the busiest airport in the world, serving 100 million passengers in 2015 alone. Residents get the perk of cheaper airline tickets and more direct flights. Plus, 83% of major U.S. cities are less than two hours away. The airport also contributes more than $34 billion in direct business revenue to the local economy.

#6. The Atlanta Beltline

This visionary use of intown Atlanta's abandoned rail path to create walkable trails has spurred economic development while connecting the city's urban neighborhoods—transforming Atlanta into a transit greenway.

#7. Hollywood of the South

Filmmakers love Atlanta, with the city serving as the location for TV's #1 rated show, "The Walking Dead" and blockbusters like "The Hunger Games." Thanks to generous tax incentives, Georgia generated more than $6 billion from film production budgets in 2014 and recently has been named the number one state for growth in the film industry.

#8. Millennial-friendly

Not only is Atlanta the #2 city in the country for millennials and the #4 city for dating, but it's also a mecca for young people looking for a quality university experience and to begin their post-college careers. It's no surprise that two in three residents of Midtown, one of the fastest-growing intown areas, are millennials.

#9. City of Neighborhoods

From historic Victorian communities to edgy and artsy enclaves to high-rise luxury apartments, Atlanta's intown neighborhoods and spacious suburban communities offer something for everyone. With tree-canopied streets and proximity to public transit, residents can enjoy a neighborhood feel with all the big-city advantages.

#10. Higher Ed Mecca

With 66 colleges offering an array of programs, including the largest concentration of historically black colleges and universities in the United States and one of the U.S.'s best engineering schools, Metro Atlanta is bubbling with students from diverse areas of study. In the 2013-14 school year, Georgia was among the top four states in the country to give the greatest amount of grant aid on a per capita basis, thanks in large part to the HOPE Scholarship.

#11. Diversity

Atlanta residents are visionary, entrepreneurial, and include a thriving creative class. Long hailed as the unofficial capital of black America, Atlanta attracts and cultivates black artists and professionals. It also is known for being LGBT-friendly, with Georgia's first high school for LGBT students and teachers slated to open in Atlanta in 2016. Many people consider Atlanta's diversity one of its greatest strengths.

INTRODUCTION
ATLANTA—THE SOUTH'S CITY

If you are energized by modern metropolises and traditional Southern charm, then Atlanta fits the bill. The South's capital city, metro Atlanta is home to more than 5.6 million people and nearly 150,000 businesses. The city offers a mix of antebellum architecture and modern glass high-rises, countless parks and rivers, and a vibrant arts, music and dining scene—not to mention having the largest aquarium in the western hemisphere and the busiest airport.

Building on its origins as a transportation crossroads, Atlanta has become a vibrant and growing community, the nation's ninth-largest metro area and home to entertainers and entrepreneurs, Fortune 500 CEOs and physicians, academics and artists.

A city of neighborhoods, Atlanta loves its festivals and historical home tours, and offers new residents many housing options from intown lofts and updated apartments to spacious homes in the burbs.

The city's turn as host to the 1996 Olympics put it on the map as a cultural and international destination, helping fuel its growth over the last two decades. But unlike other major urban centers on either U.S. coast, Atlanta offers an affordable cost of living. Your money goes further here.

In the past two decades, metro Atlanta has experienced unprecedented growth—between 2000 and 2010, it was one of only three major metros in the nation to add more than a million people (the other two cities were Houston and Dallas). Low cost of living, favorable climate, and job opportunities are all factors that spurred this growth.

The metro population grew dramatically over the last decade to 5.6 million people as of 2014. The constantly evolving downtown skyline, along with skyscrapers constructed in the Midtown, Buckhead and Perimeter (fringing I-285) business districts, reflect this growth, while the growing popularity of intown living, spurred by construction of a new transit greenway known as the Atlanta Beltline, means that Atlanta will continue to be a desirable destination for people attracted to the Southeast's fastest-growing city.

CHAPTER 1

A BRIEF HISTORY

"I have a dream that one day on the red hills of Georgia, the sons of former slaves and the sons of former slave owners will be able to sit together at the table of brotherhood."
— Martin Luther King, Jr.

A view of Grady Hospital and a horse-drawn carriage, circa 1896.

Atlanta is located in North-central Georgia at the southern tip of the Appalachians. The city's origins trace back to 1836, when Georgia decided to build a railroad to the U.S. Midwest and a location was chosen to be the line's terminus. The stake marking the founding of

15

"Terminus" was driven into the ground in 1837 (called the Zero Mile Post).

The city's birth was set in motion seven years earlier, with the government's forced resettlement of Native Americans west. The area's predominant Native American population, Cherokee and Creek, were clustered mainly in northwest Georgia. Many died on their journey on the famed Trail of Tears. Standing Peachtree, a Creek village, is now the closest Indian settlement to Atlanta.

Transportation Hub Origins

The city, which now has the world's busiest airport, has been a vital logistics and transportation center since the Civil War—its railroads made it a hub for distributing military supplies. The Union Army moved southward and invaded north Georgia in 1860. Union General William Tecumseh Sherman ordered Atlanta evacuated and burned after capturing the city on September 2, 1864. The fleeing Confederates blew up a munitions depot and set a large part of the city on fire. The fall of Atlanta was a critical point in the "war between the states."

In the aftermath of Atlanta's destruction, the city was slowly rebuilt. It helped ensure the re-election of President Abraham Lincoln and the eventual surrender of the Confederacy. By 1880, it surpassed Savannah as the state's largest city and continued to grow rapidly during the early 20th century.

Epicenter of the Civil Rights Movement

Atlanta was the focal point of the civil rights movement for four decades, and today is the fourth-largest majority black city in the country. *"It's a black-run city and probably one of the best run medium-sized cities in the nation,"* says veteran Atlanta restauranteur Dante Stephensen, who moved to Atlanta to be near Martin Luther King, Jr. at a time when King and other leaders envisioned a new South, laying the foundation for what Atlanta has become. King, along with President Jimmy Carter, received the Nobel Peace Prize, making

Atlanta one of only two cities worldwide to lay claim to two Nobel laureates.

A former marcher, Stephensen recalled when Dr. King was killed. *"Most U.S. cities had riots. In Atlanta, the blacks and whites walked arm in arm down Peachtree Street, mourning his death. Atlanta was the only major U.S. city that did not have riots."*

Rev. Martin Luther King, Jr.

For forty-three years, Stephensen owned and operated Dante's Down the Hatch, a fondue restaurant and the country's longest-running live-jazz supper club (the restaurant closed in 2013). He lives in a railway car built in 1926 and once owned by the Woolworth family.

A City Full of Energetic People with Vision

"Atlanta is a city of serendipity— people come up with ideas and do them. The city attracts a certain type of person—a person with vision," said Stephensen, pointing to the grassroots efforts of residents to save The Fox Theatre in 1974 when declining ticket sales prompted a move to close the landmark theater. A campaign, Save the Fox, started by high school students, led to 150,000 signatures and the

Long-time resident Dante Stephensen with his Samoyed, Rika

decision to place the Fox on the National Register of Historical Places.

The Fabulous Fox Theatre

Another powerful example of this grassroots activism occurred when intown communities staged demonstrations and rallies to save their neighborhoods from being decimated by plans to create overpasses and ramps to support multi-lane highways downtown. Residents opposed the Georgia Department of Transportation's move to build I-485, the Stone Mountain Freeway and Presidential Parkway through intown Atlanta.

"It was a long, protracted fight," said Dennis Mobley, president of the Inman Park Neighborhood Association. *"A number of Inman Parkers and folks from other neighborhoods banded together, creating an alliance called CAUTION Inc." he added.* CAUTION was formed to fight the Presidential Parkway as a result of former President Carter's decision to build his presidential library on the abandoned land where I-485 and the Stone Mountain Freeway intersected.

Don Bender was one of the intown activists. A Candler Park resident since 1972, Bender was living in Old Fourth Ward when the DoT tore down the house next door to him to make way for the road. During the second phase of the construction of Presidential Parkway, Bender got arrested after sitting down in front of a truck that was bringing in a crane to build a bridge over a creek near South Ponce de Leon Road.

"I have not a single regret. It was actually kind of fun," he said of his civil disobedience.

The fight extended in phases for more than thirty years, from the early 1960s until the final construction of Freedom Parkway on a small portion of the contested routes in 1994. In the process, hundreds of properties were bought by the State and torn down. Granite columns along Virginia Avenue, showing addresses of properties demolished to pave the way for the highway, are a reminder of what almost happened.

In recalling the struggle, Bender said that it went to the heart of Atlantans embracing their rights as citizens and upholding democratic ideals. *"For us, it meant that we don't let the state or the city run over the neighborhoods—that the neighborhoods are going to have a strong voice in determining their future."*

"Had residents not banded together, these neighborhoods would be dramatically different than they are today, and I don't think we'd have seen the Beltline come to fruition. A lot of things would be different today for intown Atlanta," added John Becker, former board member of the Virginia-Highland Civic Association.

Mobley said that the activism forged during the 'road fight' continues today in how active residents volunteer and serve their intown neighborhoods.

Atlanta's Olympic Dream

Another example of Atlanta's visionary spirit was when the city was selected to host the 1996 Olympic Games—an event that ushered in a business and population boom that continues to this day. Atlanta, the host city underdog, won out over Athens, Greece. Former Atlanta Mayor Andrew Young, who served as co-chair of the *Atlanta Committee for the 1996 Olympic Games*, wrote recently in a *Boston Globe* op-ed piece that having Atlanta as an Olympic host city was *"a dream I have never regretted chasing."*

Young added that he saw it as an opportunity to extend Atlanta's civil rights legacy. *"There are clearly parallel values at the heart of Coubertin's Olympic Movement—uniting the world in friendship and peace with respect for the full diversity of humanity—and the goals of the civil rights movement: to overcome discrimination through social integration and to give every human being an equal opportunity to achieve academically and economically."*

Centennial Olympic Park

Longtime writer Michelle Hiskey, in a piece in *Atlanta Magazine*, recalled how an old Southern icon, a quilt, was the symbol of the 1996 Summer Games, adorning billboards, banners, tickets—even the medals.

"It inspired the design of Centennial Olympic Park and underpinned the city's reputation for uniting across barriers of race, religion, and politics. This emblem suggested that Atlanta had connected its mishmash of ragged pieces for strength," wrote Hiskey, adding that the city needed that narrative after the Centennial Olympic park bombing. *"When Atlanta gets burned, it's in our DNA to rally and mend. The park reopened with a memorial service, and the Games marched forward,"* she wrote.

A Greener City: The Atlanta Beltline

One of Atlanta's younger visionaries is Ryan Gravel, the mastermind behind The Atlanta Beltline, a $4 billion infrastructure project first envisioned by Gravel when he was a Georgia Tech graduate student studying architecture and city planning. The project, approved in 2005 after a grassroots effort in Atlanta's intown neighborhoods, is expected to add 40% to the city's green space by converting Atlanta's abandoned 22-mile-long freight rail corridor into a "transit greenway." The first two-mile section of the Beltline opened in 2012.

Ryan Gravel on the Atlanta Beltline's Northeast Corridor

"The only reason we are doing this is because the people of Atlanta fell in love with a vision for their future," said Gravel, who was inspired to develop the Beltline concept after enjoying the walkability of Paris after living in the French capital for a year. *"What makes Atlanta really exciting is it's going to be a different place in 20 years—redefined. To be a part of that transformation is really exciting."*

CHAPTER 2
HOLLYWOOD OF THE SOUTH

Some of Atlanta's most notable residents are music entertainment royalty, from Sir Elton John to Usher, who hasn't been shy about sharing his preference for the Southeast's capital, saying, *"The beauty about living in Atlanta is that there aren't too many paparazzi here; you can just relax. And that really works for me and my children."* Thanks to a great climate, a huge variety of filming locations, and generous tax breaks from the state, the area has become a major destination for film and television production companies.

**Swan House, filming location for two of the "The Hunger Games" films.
Credit: Atlanta History Center**

The city and its outskirts frequently serve as the location for shooting some of today's biggest blockbuster films and TV shows, from the phenomenally popular zombie apocalypse TV series, "The Walking Dead," to the filming of Suzanne Collins' *Hunger Games* trilogy, earning it the nickname, Hollywood of the South. In fact, in 2014, Georgia generated more than $6 billion from film production budgets and recently has been named the number one state for growth in the film industry. The Motion Picture Association of America ranks Georgia #3 for the film industry—behind only California and New York. Some 77,900 people directly or indirectly are employed by the film industry in the state.

What's the draw? Lee Thomas, film commissioner for the State of Georgia, pointed to a number of factors. *"Georgia had a history in the film industry during the Burt Reynolds' years and the movie, 'Driving Miss Daisy'. There was already an establishment of an industry,"* said Thomas. *"We have a combination of great tax incentives and a temperate climate so filmmakers can shoot year-round. It's a diversity of locations—we have mountains, a coastline, a major metropolitan city and small towns—so they can find pretty much everything they need in Georgia. We also have a deep crew base—a lot of people in the industry live here. The twenty-six flights a day direct to Los Angeles is a huge asset. All those things together have seen Georgia really take off."*

Aspiring actress Brittney Winbush, a 2015 University of Georgia graduate, considers Atlanta the best place to pursue her acting career. She recently signed with an agent and is working with a voice and acting coach. *"In California, waitresses and police officers are all trained actors—you're not unique. In Atlanta, if you're a professionally trained actor or actress, you get to be a big fish in a little pond,"* she said.

As Thomas pointed out, the diverse landscape gives filmmakers many backdrop options, from metropolitan center to rural backwoods to suburbia. The state features a 161-kilometer coastline as well as more than 30 rivers and the Appalachian Mountains, which often get snow in the winter months. It's also cheaper to film here: Georgia gives a 20% tax credit to any film that spends a minimum of $500,000 in the state during production and an additional 10% tax credit simply for including the state logo in the rolling credits of the film.

Studios are setting up shop here, too, including the legendary British film and television giant, Pinewood Studios. It's the production company behind Marvel Studios' "Ant Man" and "Captain America 3" as well as the James Bond films. The studio, located in Fayetteville, 24 miles south of Atlanta, is expanding from 12 to 31 stages. Filmmaker Tyler Perry is building a massive movie studio on the site of Fort McPherson, located in the southwest edge of Atlanta. He received the green light to buy 330 acres of the former military base for $30 million in June 2015.

"There is a lot of excitement about the film industry; there are numerous film tourism opportunities," Lee said, pointing to her agency's own website, Come Tour Georgia, www.cometourgeorgia.com, which promotes self-guided tours for all the movies and shows shot in Georgia.

Atlanta Movie Tours' shop in Castleberry Hill.

Carrie Sagel Burns saw the potential for film tourism when she started Atlanta Movie Tours in Atlanta's "backlot," Castleberry Hill, in 2012.

"I started this company as a fan of 'The Walking Dead' so that we could give others the experiences we had right here in our backyard," recalled Burns, whose tour guides include experienced actors who have worked

on set, including zombie extras from "The Walking Dead." *"They have great stories as well as great first-hand knowledge of set-life and how to break into the industry,"* said Burns, who is working hard to ensure film tourism has a solid foundation in the city and state. *"As bigger and better movies and TV shows come to film here, so, too, come the fans of those shows. We have seen incredible growth over our three years with over 20,000 guests touring with us and many more on the horizon."*

Burns noted that besides the great opportunities to catch filming all around town, there also are opportunities to be a supplier or service provider to the entertainment industry. *"The sky's the limit; it just takes some imagination, a dream and a plan!"*

Famous Atlantans and Georgians

- Ty Cobb – baseball outfielder nicknamed "The Georgia Peach"

- Jackie Robinson – first African-American baseball player to play in the major leagues in the modern era

- Sugar Ray Robinson – boxing champion

- Martin Luther King, Jr. – Baptist minister, activist, humanitarian, and civil rights movement leader

The 39th U.S. President Jimmy Carter. Credit: Library of Congress

- Jimmy Carter – 39th President of the United States and humanitarian, awarded the 2002 Nobel Peace Prize

- Alice Walker – author of *The Color Purple*, awarded the National Book Award and the Pulitzer Prize for fiction

25

- Margaret Mitchell – author of *Gone with the Wind*, awarded the Pulitzer Prize for fiction

- Ray Charles – singer/songwriter, musician

- John C. Fremont – explorer and American military officer

- Actor Laurence Fishburne

- Radio and TV host Ryan Seacrest

- Actresses Joanne Woodward, Julia Roberts, Holly Hunter, Kim Basinger, and Dakota Fanning

- Comedian Jeff Foxworthy

CHAPTER 3

A BRIEF GEOGRAPHIC GUIDE

**Trees at their most stunning in Olmsted Linear Park.
Credit: Marc Del Santro**

Many first-time residents to Atlanta are amazed by one thing: all the trees that make the city so lush and green. Everywhere people look is an arborist's dream—magnolias, dogwoods, mimosas, Southern Yellow pines, and magnificent oaks are common. Of course, just as common are the vines, such as honeysuckle, wisteria, and kudzu, originally brought to the area for erosion control but now known widely as the "vine that ate the South."

Atlanta, located along the foothills of the Appalachians, is 132.4 square miles, the vast majority of which is dry land (less than a square mile is under water). Atlanta sits atop a ridge south of the Chattahoochee

River. Located at the far northwestern edge of the city, much of the river's natural habitat is preserved, in part due to the Chattahoochee River National Recreation Area.

The city is 1,050 feet above mean sea level, the highest major city east of the Mississippi River.

Atlanta also straddles the Eastern Continental Divide, such that rainwater that falls on the south and east side of the divide flows into the Atlantic Ocean, while rainwater on the north and west side of the divide flows into the Gulf of Mexico.

Getting Around Atlanta

**A MARTA train at Five Points Station.
Credit: MARTA**

There are a few things you need to remember about navigating Atlanta roads: one, residents love their cars and two, they love the name Peachtree. There are seventy-one streets in Atlanta with a variant of "Peachtree" in their name. In Margaret Mitchell's epic Civil War romance *Gone with the Wind*, Scarlett O'Hara lives on various points of Peachtree Street in the novel. Coincidentally, it is also where the author herself was struck by a speeding automobile, causing her death.

Very little of Atlanta is laid out in a classic north-south, east-west grid, or any grid at all for that matter. As Atlanta used to be called Terminus, in relation to its origin as a railroad settlement when it was founded as a village in 1837, many streets changed names as they went under, over or across a railroad track. However, many streets change names for seemingly no reason, which is why a smart newcomer will add the Waze app to their mobile phone before they even hit the outskirts of the city. (See more tips later in this chapter).

Atlanta's major expressways are I-75 and I-85 north /south, which merge downtown to form "The Connector," I-285 (known as "The Perimeter"), I-20 east/west, and Georgia 400 north/south. I-75, I-85 and Georgia 400 north of the city are often referred to as the Big Three in traffic reports.

A few words about getting around downtown

Downtown's new trolley – The Atlanta Streetcar.
Credit: The Atlanta Streetcar

Most areas of downtown are accessible by the city's light rail system, MARTA. There are four main rail lines: red and gold (north/south) and blue and green (east/west). All trains are labeled with the final stop of the train so commuters can easily identify routes. Check out this "Rookie Guide to Riding MARTA" video here: www.examiner. com/article/how-to-ride-marta-trains.

- Atlanta Streetcar, the 2.7-mile downtown trolley launched in 2015, was free in its first year and now costs $1 to ride as of January 2016.

- If one prefers to drive downtown, rest assured that most streets are well marked, including one-way streets. However, because very little of Atlanta is laid out on a grid, the Waze app remains a must-have navigation tool.

Navigating Atlanta Traffic

Newcomers and veterans alike hate Atlanta traffic. It's the one big negative about living here. The city's main thoroughfares and side roads slow to a crawl at peak drive times, with rush hour often beginning much earlier than typical in most cities. Atlanta highways can be deadly, too. Georgia's I-285 tops the list of the top 10 deadliest interstates in America, according to vox.com. Roadway fatalities increased from 989 in 2014 to 1,166 in 2015. There's some relief from road congestion in the summer months when school is out and many residents head to beaches and other destinations for vacation.

Advertising executive Eric Berrios has lived here for a decade and currently commutes from Acworth to Sandy Springs for work. He has a strategy for how to avoid being late and aggravated when driving: *"The rule of thumb for Atlanta is to double your expected trip travel time. If you think it's going to take an hour, let it take two."*

Six Tips for Combating Roadway Congestion

1. Live where you work or work where you live. And, never live east of where you work if you have to travel on the north end of I-285.

2. Use MARTA (Metropolitan Atlanta Rapid Transit Authority). Just leave your car at the nearest MARTA station or Park-n-Ride.

3. Work at home at least a few days a week if not full time.

4. Carpool—then you can use the HOV lane on major highways that are usually less congested.

5. Go in early and leave early to avoid the worst crush of cars on the roadways.

6. Use backroads—avoid highways if you can—or just listen to your Waze* app.

*Waze is a free, community-based traffic & navigation app where commuters in the Atlanta area post real-time updates on how to outsmart traffic, save time and improve your commute.

Click here to find Waze in the iTunes App store.

Click here to find Waze in the Android Market.

CHAPTER 4

ATLANTA'S MODERATE CLIMATE AND ENVIRONMENT

Atlantans interviewed for this book say they love the area's moderate weather. The city, founded on Peachtree Ridge, part of the Eastern Continental Divide, is located more than 1,000 feet above sea level. The high altitude cools the city off every night, even in the height of summer.

"As a Chicagoan, it gets hot in the summertime and stays hot all night. Atlanta—because of our altitude—cools down," said Dante Stephensen. A geologist by degree, Stephensen explained that the higher-than-normal altitude provides another benefit to residents—a natural barrier and safety from major catastrophes.

"Earthquakes here are rare, but most geologists predict that at some point in the future there will be a major earthquake [tsunami] in Europe. It would be devastating to our Eastern seaboard but not to us," he said.

Amazing fall foliage on the Atlanta Beltline in Old Fourth Ward. Credit: Linda Coatsworth

Atlanta native Kate Parham Kordsmeier lived in LA, Dallas and Washington, D.C., before moving back to Atlanta in September 2013. *"The weather in Atlanta is ideal because you can enjoy four true seasons—that's a far cry from living in Texas, where it is basically scorching summer ten months out of the year, or farther up north where it can get really cold,"* she said.

Hottest, Coldest Days in Atlanta

What is a typical weather day like in Atlanta? According to Weatherspark.com, an innovative weather dashboard with interactive maps and graphs, Atlanta's hottest day of the year is July 18, with an average high of 89°F, and the city's coldest day is January 18, with an average low of 32°F.

Atlanta's warm season goes from May 24 to September 19, where temperatures average a high of 82°F, and its cold season spans November 29 to February 24, during which the low tempature is a frosty 32°F and average highs don't get above 59°F.

Daily High and Low Temperature

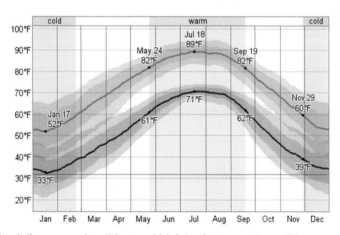

The daily average low (blue) and high (red) temperature with percentile bands (inner band from 25th to 75th percentile, outer band from 10th to 90th percentile). Courtesy of Weatherspark.com

CHAPTER 5

COST OF LIVING

According to the Metro Atlanta Chamber, the lower cost for major expenses like housing, clothing, food, and gasoline help keep Atlanta's cost of living below the U.S. average and well below those of most major metropolitan areas.

In 2013, the cost of living index in Atlanta averaged 95.3, below the national average of 100 (C2ER Cost of Living Index, 2013). That's despite the fact that the Atlanta region is now the 9th largest metro area in the nation, with a population of 5.5 million. Its quality of life and lower costs have not gone unnoticed: since 2000, metro Atlanta has grown by more than 1.1 million people—a 26 percent increase in 12 years.

Trends in Atlanta Real Median Household Income since 2005

At a Glance

Metro Population: 5,626,000

Major Industries: Financial Services, Technology, Telecommunications

Gross Metro Product: $298.5 B

Median Household Income: $56,166

Median Home Price: $177,200 (as of June 2015)

Unemployment: 5.4% (as of Oct. 2015)

Job Growth 3.5% (Oct. 2014 to Oct. 2015)

Cost of Living: up 0.5% from Oct. 2014 – Oct. 2015 (*In the United States, consumer prices were up 0.2% over that same period*)

College Attainment: 35.2%

Net Migration (2014): 14,220

Sources: U.S. Bureau of Labor Statistics, Forbes *Kiplinger

Real Median Household Income: Atlanta vs. National

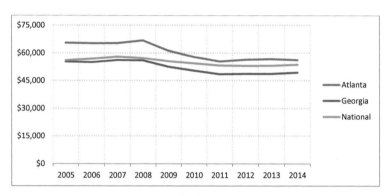

The current median household income for Atlanta is $56,166. Real median household income peaked in 2008 at $66,726 and is now $10,560 (15.83%) lower. From a post peak low of $55,411 in 2011, real median household income for Atlanta has now grown by $755 (1.36%). Source: The Census ACS 1-year survey (2014).

Utilities

Utilities are a factor in residents' cost of living and it's important to evaluate options to ensure people moving to the metro area get the best bang for their energy dollar.

While the price Atlanta pays per unit of electricity during the non-summer months is 14% to 18% lower than the national average, residents tend to pay higher electrical bills. The reason, according to one expert, is because Atlanta has less moderate temperatures than other regions as well as larger homes, requiring them to consume more energy.

"In a place like Los Angeles, people typically live in smaller spaces and the climate is moderate most of the year with less extreme variations of temperature," noted former LA resident Rob Caiello, vice president, Marketing, for Allconnect, a company that offers customers a single source to compare and connect home services through utility and energy companies representing over 50 million households and via affiliates.

Pete Marte, CEO of Hannah Solar, explained that electricity only accounts for about three-quarters of the total bill because of the Environmental Cost Compliance Recovery (ECCR) fee, construction work in progress, and state and local taxes. *"Those create a rate that is actually pretty high on a national scale,"* he said.

So, how do Atlantans' overall utility expenses (including electricity, natural gas, and TV/phone/internet) compare with other major cities? This graph provides a comparison.

City	Electricity	Natural Gas	TV/Phone/Internet Triple Play	Total
Utility and Home Services Costs For Select Cities				
Average Monthly Cost				
Boston	$104.00	$105.00	$132.00	$341.00
New York City	$108.00	$109.00	$100.00	$317.00
Chicago	$78.00	$99.00	$132.00	$309.00
Los Angeles	$94.00	$36.00	$126.00	$256.00
Atlanta	$134.00	$92.00	$129.00	$355.00
San Francisco	$90.00	$36.00	$130.00	$256.00

Sources:

- Electricity cost from US Energy Information Administration (EIA) 2014 average revenue per month per customer for: Atlanta: Georgia Power Co., Boston: NSTAR Electric Company (now Eversource), New York City: Consolidated Edison Co., Chicago: Commonwealth Edison Co., Los Angeles: Southern California Edison, San Francisco: Pacific Gas and Electric.

- Natural Gas cost from US Energy Information Administration 2014 average revenue per month per customer for the state of Georgia, Massachusetts, California, New York, and Illinois.

- Triple Play costs from internal, proprietary Allconnect, Inc. 2014-15 customer purchase data.

"There are numerous choices and options out there and people need to do their homework," advised Caiello. *"At Allconnect.com, people can enter their address and compare current pricing from cable, satellite, high-speed internet, home phone, gas and electricity providers in their area."*

Natural Gas Marketers

One of the most unique aspects of utilities in the Peach State is that natural gas is completely deregulated so residents can select their natural gas provider. *"Understanding how natural gas works in Georgia and what you can expect is really important,"* said Caiello.

The Georgia Public Service Commission provides an approved list of gas marketers with contact information at: www.psc.state.ga.us/gas/certified_marketers.asp. As of October 2015, there were 13 providers.

Electric Utilities: Home to Nation's Largest Number of EMCs

When it comes to electricity providers, half of Georgia's 9.4 million residents rely on one of the state's forty-two electric membership corporations (EMCs). According to *GEORGIA Magazine*, Georgia boasts the largest number of electric cooperative members of any state in the country.

Georgia Power Company provides electricity to most of Atlanta inside the Perimeter (statewide, they serve 2.4 million people). Other suburban communities use an EMC or municipally owned electric system. Today, eight EMCs currently serve metro Atlanta, mostly in Cobb and Gwinnett counties, as well as residents in Cherokee, Douglas, Fayette, Henry, and Rockdale counties. A few communities like the City of Marietta operate their own municipal electrical service.

Caiello urges new residents to look at all their options to help sort through the complexities of the different packages and find the best one. Allconnect offers quotes from up to seven of the 13 gas marketers in Atlanta on the website, www.gasgeorgia.com.

"I also recommend that you get to know your electricity provider," said Caiello, noting that Georgia Power, for example, offers tools to help residents track their energy usage. Homeowners can schedule a free energy audit at their house, where an expert will tour each room and offer tips for reducing power usage and saving money.

Solar Energy Tax Credit

One way to save on energy expenses long-term is to install a solar system on the roof. According to Marte of Hannah Solar, solar systems have come down in price in Georgia, with the average system running $15,000 compared with $30,000 a few years ago. He added that it takes 10 to 12 years before the system pays for itself and begins to save consumers money. New homeowners should know that the 30 percent residential tax credit on solar systems on residential homes is in effect through the end of December 2019 after Congress passed an extension of the Solar Investment Tax Credit.

Atlantans also have the option to lease solar. Solar Power Rocks, www. solarpowerrocks.com/georgia, is a resource to learn more about leasing and finding local installers in the area.

Marte recommends that residents get at least two quotes from qualified installers. Questions to ask before investing in a system include:

1. Do you have references from your solar installer?

2. How much space do you have to put solar on? Specifically, how much space faces southeast, southwest or south?

3. How old is your roof? If your roof is older than seven or eight years, you may want to re-roof before putting up the system.

4. How old is your home's electrical system? Is it up to code? Be sure to work with a licensed electrician to ensure all electrical is up to code before the system is installed.

Electric Vehicle-friendly

**Two vehicles plug in at a Level 2 charging station at City Hall, Roswell Ga.
Credit: Jeff Cohen, AEVDC**

While a generous tax credit has gone away for residents who buy all-electric vehicles (EVs), a move that threatens Georgia's status as the #2 state for EVs, Atlanta remains friendly to eco-minded drivers given the number of charging stations in place around the metro area. Jeff Cohen, founder, Atlanta Electric Vehicle Development Coalition, cited a Department of Energy report that states there are now more than 630 charging ports in Georgia, mostly in the metro area.

"The good news is if you are bringing an electric vehicle into Atlanta or you want to buy one, you will find it's very convenient to charge your EV because the city and the state have continued to invest in charging station infrastructure," said Cohen, adding that there are just under 23,000 EVs now registered in the state.

Unfortunately, EV drivers have to pay more to register their car here (fees have jumped from $85 to $200 to cover lost gas tax income). Cohen said Atlantans are still eligible for a federal tax credit on a new

EV purchase, valued at up to $7,500 based on their vehicle's battery size.

And, they can hop onto the HOV lane even as a single rider, which is not insigificant given Atlanta's infamous traffic.

Property Taxes in Georgia and the Metro Atlanta Area

According to WalletHub, an online news site designed to help consumers and small business owners make better financial decisions, the average American household spends $2,089 on property taxes for their homes each year. Where does Georgia stack up in terms of property taxes compared with other U.S. states? Georgia ranked dead middle—twenty-fifth in the country—with an average property tax bill of $1,675, based on WalletHub's 2015 analysis of states with the highest and lowest property taxes.

The Minnesota Center for Fiscal Excellence ranked the largest fifty cities for the amount of homestead property taxes homowners paid for a $150,000 property in 2014. The table below shows where Atlanta ranked compared with other major cities (amount shown includes assessment limits).

City	Net Tax	Ranking
2014 Average Homestead Property Tax in Select Cities ($150K Value)		
Atlanta	$1,855.00	#29
Detroit	$5,218.00	#2
Chicago	$2,453.00	#18
Las Vegas	$1,696.00	#33
New York City	$905.00	#50
Washington, D.C.	$650.00	#51
Houston	$2,809.00	#15
Philadelphia	$1,592.00	#35
Los Angeles	$1,075.00	#46

Sources: Lincoln Institute; Minnesota Center for Fiscal Excellence, 50 State Property Tax Study, 2014.

CHAPTER 6
SERVICES

Vehicle Registration

New Georgia residents will have thirty days to register their car in the state. They will need their driver's license, proof of insurance, proof of residency, a completed Title/Tag Application, and proof of passed vehicle emissions inspection (if applicable).

Residents also must apply for a Georgia driver's license within thirty days of residency, prior to registering their vehicle. The good news: a lot of this can be done online before visiting a customer service center. Go to www.online.dds.ga.gov/onlineservices/preapply.

Most centers in the metro Atlanta area offer appointments to transfer an out-of-state license. As long as an out-of-state license is current and surrendered at the time of a new resident's motor vehicle appointment, no written exam will be required.

How Safe is Atlanta?

Anyone moving to Atlanta needs to do their homework about crime and safety, especially when looking at certain neighborhoods. *"Atlanta is a city that suffers from crime and it's on par with any other large city in America,"* said Volkan Topalli, professor of Criminal Justice at Georgia State University. Topalli researches violence in urban settings, and has conducted roughly 400 interviews with street offenders in New

Orleans, St. Louis, and Atlanta over the past 12 years. Atlanta, like many major cities in America, grapples with crime problems brought about by economic and justice disparities, the GSU professor said.

"Policing in Atlanta has been steadily improving over the last 20 years not only in terms of how open law enforcement is to new techniques and strategies, but also in terms of how they reach out to the community."

Atlanta Senior Police Officer W. Crane

Topalli said residents driving through the City of Atlanta in the course of four or five blocks will pass through the jurisdictions of the Georgia State University Police Department, the Atlanta Police Department, the Georgia Capital Police Department, the MARTA Police Department, the Fulton County Sheriff's Office, and numerous federal agencies such as the Department of Homeland Security.

"That makes for a very complex, complicated kind of structure for policing. Some of that comes from the history of Georgia having a very localized form of governance," he said. The disadvantage, however, is that police departments don't share resources and infrastructure to control crime or the movement of crime.

Because Atlanta is a city of neighborhoods, there is a strong tradition of community policing and locally engaged law enforcement. The city is divided into twenty-five Neighborhood Planning Units or NPUs, which are citizen advisory councils that make recommendations to the Mayor and City Council on zoning, land use and other planning issues. The NPU system was established in 1974 to provide an opportunity for citizens to participate actively in the Comprehensive Development Plan. The system enables citizens to express ideas and comment on city plans and proposals while assisting the city in developing plans that best meet the needs of their communities.

Residents use NPUs to address issues like crime. Topalli explained that the individual chances someone moving to a new area will experience crime is still "very small" even in cities with high crime rates. He added that serious street crime in any city is carried out by a very small percentage of the population.

"Atlanta has a tremendous amount going for it—it's a city where there is a lot of entrepreneurial activitiy and where people take chances and risks both in terms of where they establish businesses and where they live. Things move very fast here and with that comes a certain amount of uncertainty, including in crime," he said.

Since the mid-1990s, crime has been dropping in Georgia, with incidents of violent crime declining almost 25% from the years 2000 through 2012. Breaking it down further, murder and non-negligent manslaughter decreased almost 24%, forcible rape decreased over 10%, robbery decreased over 22%, and aggravated assault decreased over 27%. In addition, incidents of property crime are down almost 20%, with the most dramatic drop in motor vehicle theft, which decreased by over 39%.

The Reports also indicated that, in 2012, the violent crime rate in Georgia was about 2% lower than the national average. However, the property crime rate was over 19% higher than the national average.

Here's how Atlanta compares with other major metropolitan areas in three key crime categories: aggravated assault, burglary and auto theft in 2014:

Metro Area	Population	Burglary		Assault		Car T
2014 Data	Total*	Total	Per 100K	Total	Per 100K	Total
Atlanta	5.6	40,636	725.9	12,198	217.9	18,749
Chicago	7.3	26,809	365.2	16,315	222	13,720
New York City	14.2	29,998	209.7	37,845	264.5	12,227
Philadelphia	6.1	26,152	432.0	14,448	239	9,529
Washington, D.C.	6.0	15,682	260.0	10,013	166	11,161

Source: FBI Uniform Crime Reports (2014). *Total population figures in millions.

No More Public Housing

One change in Atlanta that affected crime levels was eliminating low-income housing, which occurred in 2011 when housing projects were demolished and residents received housing vouchers, said Topalli. *"Atlanta was the first city in America to have public housing and it's also the first city in America to have completely removed it."*

"Initially there was a drop in crime since most crime in Atlanta was not gang oriented but was associated with housing projects," he said. *"A lot of people moved south of the city to Cleveland Avenue or Clayton County, and there's been a slight increase in crime recently due to the fact that these offenders have re-established their crime territories,"* he explained.

Atlanta's Healthcare Landscape

Metro Atlanta is home to a number of well-established hospitals and prominent healthcare assets, including the Centers for Disease Control and Prevention, the national headquarters of the American Cancer Society, CARE International and a host of university medical schools, from Emory University to Morehouse School of Medicine. Atlanta also is a cluster for healthcare IT firms (read more in the Economy chapter). What does this mean for residents? *"It tends to foster a culture of innovation that indirectly filters down to the consumer,"* said veteran health journalist Andy Miller, who started Georgia Health News, a non-profit news site that covers healthcare across the state, in 2010.

Forbes recently ranked Northside Hospital the 23rd best employer in America.
Credit: Daniel Piper

Insurance Choice

Residents will find that most major health insurance providers are in Atlanta, including Aetna, United Healthcare, Kaiser Permanente, and Blue Cross/Blue Shield of Georgia, which is the largest in the state and insures approximately one in three people in Georgia.

Because Georgia doesn't operate a state insurance exchange, with the state taking a *"very hands-off approach,"* according to Miller, new residents must use the federal exchange to shop for health insurance if their company doesn't offer them a plan. Open enrollment for the Health Insurance Marketplace generally runs every year from November 1 through mid-December, while changes or enrollments to start March 1st are typically due by Jan. 31.

New residents to Georgia can get health insurance on the Marketplace outside of the open enrollment period if they have a qualifying life event. Examples include moving to a new state, certain changes in income, and changes in family size. Residents have sixty days from the event to sign up or change coverage (though Native Americans and people who qualify for Medicaid can enroll anytime during the year.). HealthCare.gov is the best online resource for subsidized health insurance sold in the Affordable Care Act Marketplace.

Snapshot of Atlanta's Major Hospitals and Health Systems

The Georgia Association for Primary Health Care outlines metro Atlanta's four large health care systems and their geographic focus this way:

WellStar Health System – primary provider in the northwestern suburbs

Northside Hospital – serves north Atlanta communities from its hub at 1-285 and Ga. 400, with hospitals in Cherokee and Forsyth counties.

Piedmont Healthcare – has a high-profile campus in the heart of Atlanta, as well as a major presence across the south side of the metro area with hospitals in Fayette and Henry counties and in Newnan in Coweta County.

Emory Healthcare – known for its locations on the Emory University campus east of Atlanta and for its Midtown hospital, it also sprawls into Johns Creek to the north, Tucker further to the east, Smyrna to the north and west, and thanks to its partnership with Emory St. Joseph, to the top end of the Perimeter.

Atlantans call part of the I-285 / 400 corridor in Sandy Springs "Pill Hill." It's increasingly recognized as the healthcare mecca of Atlanta, with three hospitals, hundreds of physician practices, multiple outpatient centers and support services.

Additional area hospitals and health systems beyond these big four include Grady Memorial Hospital in Atlanta, Dekalb Medical, Gwinnett Medical Center (which is getting ready to merge with Northside Hospital) and Atlanta Medical Center. WellStar just announced it is buying the five Tenet hospitals in Georgia, including Atlanta Medical Center, which will make it the largest health system in the state.

New residents can research hospitals and doctors through HealthGrades.com. The Leapfrog Group's Hospital Safety Score (www. hospitalsafetyscore.org) also is a very reliable place for consumers to get information about local hospital safety scores. In addition, several local publications, including *Atlanta Magazine* and *Georgia Trend*, publish annual lists of the best hospitals in the city. Here is a link to the most recent national ranking of the Best Hospitals in Atlanta by *U.S. News and World Report*: www.health.usnews.com/best-hospitals/ area/atlanta-ga.

One recent study doesn't put the Peach State in the best light when it comes to access and cost of care. The non-profit Commonwealth Fund released its 2015 scorecard of state health system performance, and the state of Georgia was ranked among the unhealthiest states, dropping from 45th to 46th nationally. However, 11 of 13 indicators improved for Georgia. In addition, uninsured rates dropped significantly. The scorecard included health system performance in areas such as healthcare access and affordability.

Lack of Price Transparency

A downside to Georgia's healthcare scene, Miller said, is a lack of price transparency for medical services. *"The price for an MRI could vary from $400 to $1,400 depending on the facility,"* he said.

Going to an in-network facility doesn't mean that the providers working in those facilities are in-network, which means that residents could get a separate doctor bill that is not covered by their insurance.

More Georgians are Uninsured

Data from the U.S. Census bureau finds that more Georgians had health insurance in 2014 than in 2013, yet the state still ranked fourth-highest in the most number of uninsured residents at 15.8 percent; only Texas, Alaska and Florida had a higher rate of uninsured.

"One of the problems we have in Georgia is the high percentage of residents who have no health insurance," said Miller. *"Much of that has to do with the state not expanding Medicaid under the Affordable Care Act."* The insured *"pay indirectly for the uninsured through higher bills and premiums,"* he added. A portion of the property taxes in Fulton and DeKalb counties goes to the Grady Health System to cover the uninsured in those counties.

Physician Practices

Word-of-mouth recommendations from other residents are always the best way to find physicians and other healthcare practitioners in any city. Newcomers can also use online research to narrow their search. Every July, *Atlanta Magazine* publishes its Top Doctors rankings—the doctors whom other doctors trust most. To search the magazine's Top Doctors database, you need to be an *Atlanta Magazine Insider*. Sign-up is free. Go to: www.atlantamagazine.com/register/#register.

A quick Google search found 613 pediatric specialists in the Atlanta area on HealthGrades.com. The site includes patient satisfaction ratings. Residents can fine-tune their search by practicing specialties, conditions treated, procedures performed, and whether the doctor is board certified or has no sanctions. Atlantans can search using additional criteria such as distance from their home, gender and the type of insurance accepted.

Hospice Care

Atlanta residents can receive hospice in a home, in a long-term care facility, or in some instances, at an inpatient hospice facility. To qualify for hospice care, a medical doctor has to determine that a person is in the end stage of his or her disease with no hope of a cure and has six months or less to live. Like palliative care, hospice care requires a referral from a physician and an evaluation.

Metro Atlanta offers many options for families needing hospice care for a loved one. Paula Sanders, executive director of Georgia Hospice and Palliative Care Organization, said there are about thirty-five to fifty providers in the metro Atlanta area at any given time. *"The number of providers in Atlanta can change as a result of consolidation in the industry. That's why it can be tough for anybody to navigate,"* she said, adding that certain providers are better known for working closely with assisted living and nursing home facilities, while others are predominantly home-based.

GHPCO provides a searchable map to find member providers at: www.ghpco.memberclicks.net/find-a-provider. Region four covers the metro area. Atlanta residents also can search for hospice providers at this state site: www.gamap2care.info/Locator.html#.

Community Blood Centers

Metro Atlanta's blood needs are served predominantly by two non-profit community blood supplier organizations—the American Red Cross and LifeSouth. LifeSouth is a blood supplier for more than 100 hospitals in Alabama, Florida, and Georgia. It has three Georgia locations: Dunwoody, outside the Perimeter in northeast Atlanta, serves as a hub for LifeSouth, while two collection sites are located in McDonough and Gaineseville.

The American Red Cross is the country's single largest supplier of blood, and has the only national network of blood collection and distribution centers. While local hospital needs are met first, the Red Cross is committed to ensuring all hospital patients throughout the country have blood when and where they need it.

Donors can find donation opportunities by visiting redcrossblood. org, calling 1-800-RED CROSS (1-800-733-2767) or using the Red Cross Blood Donor App.

Veterans Service

Nearly one million active duty, reserve, guard, and veterans live in Georgia, making the Peach State the fifth in the nation for the number of both active duty military and female veterans. The Atlanta VA Medical Center in Decatur is one of three medical facilities in the state serving veterans. The VA offers several transportation options, including door-to-door rides for up to forty miles for older vets who qualify for the service.

Nursing Home Care

Georgia veterans who need nursing care facilities have the option of two nursing homes, where they can stay for a nominal charge:

Georgia War Veterans Nursing Home at Augusta

Georgia War Veterans Home at Milledgeville

For more information on all the veteran-related services, visit the Georgia Department of Veterans Service website at veterans.georgia. gov or call 404-656-2300. A full list of the offices on an interactive map can be found here: www.veterans.georgia.gov/field-offices. Residents can visit www.veterans.georgia.gov/satellite-locations to find a satellite location nearest them.

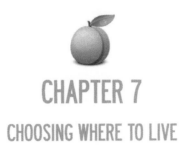

CHAPTER 7

CHOOSING WHERE TO LIVE

"The housing market is strong in Atlanta. It's a seller's market, especially in certain areas." – Linda Mattingly, President, Hometura real estate firm

Economic Outlook for Housing

Housing prices are rebounding in Atlanta. According to Kiplinger, in 2014, Atlanta was among the top cities that experienced double-digit price growth, trailing only Detroit and cities in California, but surpassing the growth in housing markets in both Miami and Las Vegas.

As of June 2015, the median home sale price in metro Atlanta was $177,500, 8.6% higher than a year ago but still 20.3% lower than mid-2006, when the real estate bubble was at its peak. Nationally, home prices rose an average of 5.2%. This data, reported in Kiplinger, was tracked by Clear Capital, a provider of real estate data and analysis.

Kiplinger's findings echo what local real estate agents say about the Atlanta market. *"Home values have come back to pre-2008 levels and some communtiies have surpassed that,"* said Linda Mattingly, president of Hometura, a realtor firm based in Brookhaven. *"Right now there are more buyers than there is property."*

That's especially true for in-demand locations closer to downtown and suburban communities with excellent schools. Mattingly's advice for anyone looking to move to Atlanta is to think about traffic: *"The quality of life for their family is the location of their new home and it may not be where you work, but where the schools and activities are.*" She advises that before purchasing or leasing a home, to drive the route to and from work during an actual work day to get a realistic picture of the traffic.

Dual-career couple Christian Toulet and Cindy Herrera relocated to Atlanta from Arizona in early 2015 and initially rented in Roswell. *"I'm glad we did—especially not knowing the market or the area in general and where I was going to be working,"* said Herrera.

By summer, they began looking to buy a home in the East Cobb, Sandy Springs or Smyrna area to get closer to Herrera's work. *"The market got hot really fast,"* said Toulet, who was looking for a bit more land and very open floor plans.

"We would find the right home, make an offer and we were outbid from the get-go," said Herrera.

The couple opted in the end to buy new construction. Toulet observed that developers are already looking at price increases for new homes, a further indication of the housing market recovery. Their advice? Rent first and learn the Atlanta market. *"It would have been a really different story had we purchased something in this area and then found out how bad Atlanta traffic is,"* said Herrera.

The tables below show the largest residential real estate firms and several that specialize in the intown market.

	Atlanta's Top 10 Residential Real Estate Organizations
1	Keller Williams Realty, Southeast Region
2	RE/MAX of Georgia, Inc.
3	Harry Norman Realtors
4	BHHS Georgia Properties
5	Coldwell Banker Real Estate, LLC
6	Atlanta Fine Homes Sotheby's International Realty
7	Better Homes and Gardens Real Estate Metro Brokers
8	Solid Source Real Estate Cos.
9	Atlanta Community Real Estate Brokerage LLC
10	Chapman Hall Realtors, Inc.

Source: *Atlanta Business Chronicle*, March 6, 2015.

Firms Specializing in Intown Listings	
Adams Realty	Holley Realty
Alma Fuller	Homestead Real Estate
Avenue Realty	Intown Expert Realty
Coldwell Banker	Karafotias Realty
DJK Realty	Keller Knapp
Engel & Volkers	Keller Williams
Golley Realty	Red Robin Realtors
Harry Norman	Re/Max Metro Atlanta

Key Neighborhoods inside the Perimeter

Intown living continues to grow in popularity to Atlantans with many pluses, from the strong sense of community in many of Atlanta's historic and eclectic neighborhoods to the walkability, access to shopping, dining, and cultural venues and proximity to downtown. Of course, every person has to weigh the pluses with the negatives of intown living (the three most commonly cited are traffic, parking issues, and crime.).

Below are spotlights on some of Atlanta's most interesting established and emerging intown communities with insights on what make them unique from the residents who live there. Because of space constraints, this book was unable to feature every neighborhood.

Ansley Park

Ansley Park, one of Atlanta's most affluent communities, is the second-oldest neighborhood in Atlanta and once housed the Georgia Governor's Mansion before it was torn down in 1969. Homes range in price from $150,000 for a one-bedroom condo to $4 million for a five-bedroom, 7,700 square-foot house.

"*The stately homes, curvy roads, and mature hardwood trees give Ansley a timeless charm, yet we can see the skyscrapers of Midtown from our front porch,*" said Eric Champlin, who bought a condo in Ansley Park in

2011. Champlin said the neighborhood's proximity to Piedmont Park was a huge draw for him, as well as Ansley's five parks that daisy chain through the community.

George Washington "Wash" Collier was the original land owner. His house remains today in Ansley Park and is the oldest house in Atlanta still standing where it was originally built. Edwin Ansley, a developer, purchased the land at auction after Collier's death.

**The Ansley Park Historic District is located in Midtown, west of Piedmont Park.
Credit: Eric Champlin**

Corporate executives transferring to Atlanta consider Ansley very desirable, given its proximity to nightlife and cultural events. Residents enjoy playing golf year-round at the Ansley Golf Club, Atlanta's second-oldest country club. *Sports Illustrated* rated it the second best nine-hole layout in America.

Gordon Smith, owner of a video production company, has lived in Ansley since 1977 and enjoyed the neighborhood's golf amenities for most of that time.

"It is one of the charms of the neighborhood," he said, noting that the club would run a van to members' houses to pick up children and bring them over to the club. Smith said that the golf club has always

been very conscious of the neighborhood, reaching out and working with the residents. That's a good thing, he explained since the land is held in trust, meaning that the golf course and neighborhood are here to stay.

The Ansley Golf Course's view of Hole #1 from tee to green.
Credit: Ansley Golf Course

The neighborhood holds Friday night potluck dinners in one of the parks during summer. A "restaurant travelers' group" visits eateries around town, while the neighborhood's diners' club members take turns hosting meals in their homes. Ansley Park residents also enjoy book, gardening, and bridge clubs. *"It's a really active neighborhood,"* Champlin said.

Avondale Estates

Avondale Estates, a peaceful community located eight miles east of Atlanta, is the only documented example of a planned city in the Southeast. George Francis Willis, a millionaire who earned his fortune selling pharmaceuticals in the 1920s, established the city in 1924. His plans were inspired by a trip he and his wife took to Stratford-upon-Avon, England, the birthplace of William Shakespeare, where he recreated the majestic Tudor-Revival style architecture.

Lake Avondale in picturesque Avondale Estates.
Credit: City of Avondale Estates

Located next door to Decatur, Avondale Estates features a lake, plenty of lush trees (it's the second-oldest designated "tree city" in the state), and the only museum school in Georgia. The curriculum is built on the museum model that fosters exploration and discovery; the school partners with museums and other learning institutions to provide real-life experiences with classroom topics. The charter school started in 2010 by the First Baptist Church in Avondale Estates now has more than five hundred students. Property prices range from $90,000 for a two-bedroom house to $785,000 for a four-bedroom home, while condos are available for as low as $56,000 or as high as $270,000.

Residents enjoy a strong sense of community and easy access to downtown Atlanta. They range in age from millennials to young families to retirees. The City is home to the original Waffle House, which opened in 1955 on College Avenue and has since been converted into a museum.

Community events include the Avondale Estates AutumnFest Arts & Music Festival, held in October and free to the public, and the Christmas Tour of Homes and Holiday Market held annually in December. For the holiday tours, trolleys transport guests to six of the City's most interesting homes.

The Rail Art District (RAD) Studio Cruise is held annually in March along the CSX rail line running through Avondale Estates, east Decatur, and Scottdale. This free event offers attendees the opportunity to travel to the different participating art studios by trolley. The participating studios offer performances, demonstrations, and art items for purchase.

City Manager Clai Brown considers his favorite event Avondale's 4th Of July celebration, beginning with a parade through downtown in the morning and culminating with music bands and fireworks at Lake Avondale.

"It's one big party—like Mardi Gras—thousands gather and there isn't any green visible around the lake," said the eight-year city manager who lives just two blocks from the house he grew up in in Avondale Estates. *"Back then, locals called the city "Mayberry,"—neighbors knew each other and left their doors unlocked,"* recalled Brown.

"That sense of community is still here. People are always out and walking around the lake." His late father, Dewey Brown, was city manager and police chief in Avondale Estates for forty-six years.

What would Brown tell people thinking about moving to Avondale? *"It's a wonderful place to live and raise a family. We are conveniently located just ten minutes from downtown. Emory, Decatur, DeKalb Medical, Georgia Tech, Georgia State, Oglethorpe, and Hartsfield Jackson Airport are all nearby. We are a community—people know each other and help each other out. Avondale is something special."*

Brookhaven

**Town Brookhaven;
Credit: R. Sargent**

Brookhaven, a community of 50,000 residents, is inside the Perimeter between Buckhead and Chamblee. Developed in 1910, the Brookhaven Historic District is the oldest planned golf course and country club residential community in Georgia. The community also has a lake, wooded areas, and the Capital City Clubhouse.

"Brookhaven is very diverse," said Doug Mandel, owner of a media sales company, who lives with his wife, Kathryn, and son in a renovated 1930s-era home that is on the National Register of Historical Places. *"Even though a lot of houses have been renovated, it's still a truly unique historical neighborhood with a lot of character,"* he added.

A class convenes on the quad at Oglethorpe University's historic Gothic campus in Brookhaven. Credit: Oglethorpe University

Brookhaven became DeKalb County's eleventh city in late 2012. Town Brookhaven is a state-of-the-art mixed-use development situated on Peachtree Road, north of Lenox Square Mall and Phipps Plaza and adjacent to historic Oglethorpe University, a private liberal arts college with its own art museum. Built six years ago, Town Brookhaven has a host of theaters, galleries, and trendy restaurants. The emerging Brookhaven Village along Dresden Drive is highly walkable with several luxury apartments close to MARTA and popular with young couples and singles.

Housing prices range from a two-bedroom condo for as low as $170,000 to a five-bedroom estate home for $2.2 million.

"The one thing that makes Brookhaven unique, besides being a very active community, is its location—you are minutes from I-85, I-285 and GA

400. You're five minutes from a hospital. It's a great location," said Linda Mattingly, a real estate agent who moved to Brookhaven in 1993 from Dallas, Texas.

Community-wide events include the just-launched Cherry Blossom Festival, held in March at Blackburn Park, and the Brookhaven Arts Festival held in the fall. Every Thursday from June through early August, Brookhaven "Movies on the Town," takes place in the community green space at Town Brookhaven.

Buckhead

**The "Beverly Hills of the East," Buckhead is a thriving business center with upscale dining and shopping.
Courtesy: Buckhead Coalition**

This affluent uptown district of Atlanta *"is Atlanta business,"* said Buckhead Business Association member Michael Crandal, a management leadership consultant and motivational speaker, who moved to Buckhead a few years ago from Palm Springs, CA, when his wife accepted a new position in the hospitality sector. *"Buckhead is probably the most vibrant, economically sound community in the entire United States right now,"* he added, pointing to the number of high-rise apartment buildings being erected, which are "creating a 'new' skyline seemingly every 90 days."

Crandal explained that the vast majority of Buckhead developments are for apartments, not condos, to appeal to younger workers who aren't ready to make a down payment on a condo or home. A few examples include SkyHouse, Cyan on Peachtree, and Crescent Terminus, all offering over 300 units at prices ranging as low as $1128 for a studio to the high end of $4885 for a three-bedroom luxury apartment. On the other end of the spectrum, Buckhead condos on the top floors of the St. Regis Hotel and Mandarin Hotel go for $3 million to $5 million apiece and are selling, said Crandal.

According to the history page on buckhead.net, the community traces its origin to Henry Irby's general store and tavern, which was founded in 1837. Situated at present-day West Paces Ferry Road and Roswell Road, Irby's tavern became the stopping place for travelers in the sparsely populated wilderness. Irby killed a large deer and mounted the "buck head" where travelers could see it. The name Buckhead stuck and a campaign in the late 19th century to rename the area Northside Park was unsuccessful.

Buckhead has come a long way from its frontier origins. Known as "The Beverly Hills of the East," it is considered the premier destination for shopping and fine dining in Atlanta, with hundreds of restaurants and two high-end malls, Lenox Square and Phipps Plaza. There is even a new NBC drama called "Buckhead" being shot around town, which has been dubbed *a drama about ambition, sex, and revenge set in the extravagant, high-stakes world of Atlanta politics, entertainment, churches, and strip clubs,*" reports *Creative Loafing Atlanta.*

According to Crandal, *"The hospitality industry plays a major role in Buckhead as both a top employer and contributing to the uniqueness of the city as a whole."*

Civic and business groups include Buckhead Rotary Club and Buckhead Business Association. The nearby Atlanta History Center features one of the Southeast's largest history museums, two historic houses, and the Centennial Olympic Games Museum.

The walkability of Buckhead remains a major draw for the Crandals. *"From where we live we can walk to any of twenty restaurants, three groceries, a pharmacy, and three different movie theaters,"* said Crandal. *"We came here with two cars and got rid of one of them because we didn't need it."*

Castleberry Hill

Castleberry Hill, one of Atlanta's premier art districts.

One of Atlanta's premier art districts, Castleberry Hill is often identified as the lone wolf of intown neighborhoods because of its geographic isolation. It borders MLK to the north, Spring Street to the east, McDaniel to the south, and Northside Drive to the west.

It is separated from south Atlanta neighborhoods by a railroad, bridges, and "the Gulch," a P-shaped undeveloped area situated at ground level that the city erected a century ago. Streets that surround the Gulch are elevated to enable traffic to more easily flow above the railroad lines passing through downtown Atlanta.

"This community has always been off the beaten path," noted Carrie Burns, president of the Castleberry Hill Neighborhood Association. *"Atlanta's railroad ended in Terminus, which is the corner of our neighborhood at MLK and Spring,"* she said.

While home prices in the trendy loft business district are increasing, home shoppers can pick up a one-bedroom house for as low as $118,000. On the high end, a three-bedroom home goes for $2.5 million.

Burns considers the neighborhood's location a major asset. Residents are a ten-minute walk to Centennial Olympic Park. From there they can catch the Atlanta Streetcar to get to other locations, including Edgewood. The neighborhood is *"extremely dog friendly,"* and has a surprising number of babies and young children, she added. It's also a five to ten-minute walk to a MARTA station, which can transport residents quickly all around the city.

Parking, like all of intown Atlanta, remains the biggest challenge.

"Atlanta is not public-transit-oriented enough to make it super pedestrian-friendly—that's why we are still so reliant on our cars all over the city," Burns said.

According to an article from *Atlanta Magazine*, Castleberry Hill was, by the mid-nineteenth century, a red-light district filled with prostitutes, gambling, and cockfighting. Speakeasies also were prevalent. Back in the city's railroad heyday in the 1850s, it was called "Snake Nation"—the name given to a renegade community that thrived there.

"It was a fringe group of artists—people who were bucking the system," noted Burns, expressing a wish that the neighborhood reclaim its old name.

The federally recognized historic district and loft-rich community has come a long way from its illustrious early history. *"What I love about it is that it's done, but there is so much we can do with more green and community space,"* said Burns, who has lived in Castleberry Hill for fifteen years.

Back in 2001, she was looking to buy a loft and considered properties as far north as Buckhead and pretty far south of downtown until deciding on her current home. *"I wanted a loft that was raw but not so raw that I would have to develop it on my own; I wanted something safe and something in my price range."* She noted she wasn't the earliest to move to Castleberry Hill; earlier waves of people began moving into the area in 1988 and later in 1996 coinciding with the Atlanta Summer Olympic Games.

Among the earliest group of arrivals were Calvin Lockwood and Steve Messer, who own the Granite Room. The space originally was a dry goods store and chicken hatchery on Peters Street and has now been converted into a gallery, event space, photography studio, and their home.

Burns said that by the time she arrived in 2001, some of the first restaurants and retail establishments began to open, while photography studios and art galleries started to come in. The Goat Farm Arts Center, an urban arts space housed in industrial buildings in historic West End, has started investing in the area and now has studios in Castleberry Hill.

No Mas! Cantina in Castleberry Hill.

Today, Castleberry Hill has over eighty businesses, includes No Mas! Cantina/Hacienda, which serves some of the city's best Mexican cuisine and has amazing jewelry, home goods, and gifts from Mexican artisans, and The Smoke Ring, a contemporary barbeque restaurant whose chef and owner Jordan Wakefield won Food Networks' "Guy's Grocery Games."

Burns predicts that by 2017 there will be well over a hundred businesses and easily three hundred more residents, based on projected developments coming in as well as the Hard Rock Hotel Atlanta set to open in spring 2018.

"Most people don't realize that every single building in Castleberry is a residence," she said. *"You have everything from $80,000 studios to $5 million lofts here."*

The neighborhood association holds a monthly meeting and a social (happy hour), as well as a loft tour and chili cook-off in the fall. In the spring there is oftentimes an arts festival. One of the main community events is the Art Stroll held every second Friday. Often area restaurants offer specials. And the galleries may hold an art show opening or serve wine to encourage people to come out.

Burns said more events will be coming once Castleberry gets its community space. An $80,000 grant is funding that project, which will be "partially a soccer field and partially a meeting space."

"Our community space will be used for artist markets, craft markets, and during the Art Stroll it will be a great place to set up a little market or have live music," she explained, adding that soccer is so popular in the neighborhood that it spurred the 2015 creation of a new non-profit, the Castleberry Hill Athletic Club. Another development that promises to add more foot traffic to Castleberry Hill is the new Mercedes Benz Stadium, future home of the Atlanta Falcons, being built and scheduled for completion by first quarter 2017. Burns said most residents view the stadium as a positive.

Decatur

Comprising just over four square miles, Decatur is situated east of midtown Atlanta and west of Stone Mountain. The county seat of DeKalb County, this historic city was founded in 1823, before neighboring Atlanta.

Centered on the historic DeKalb County Courthouse, Decatur has become a hot destination for college students and young professionals who want hip bars, great restaurants, and walkable neighborhoods, as well as for families who are drawn to the excellent independent school district. There are three-bedroom homes priced at $60,000 as well as five-bedroom homes that go for $1.2 million, or $770,000 for a luxury three-bedroom condo.

Enjoying the atmosphere of Decatur Square on Sycamore Street.
Credit: City of Decatur

Nearby employers include Emory University (which runs a shuttle for employees in Decatur ever day) and Centers for Disease Control and Prevention, in addition to women's liberal arts school, Agnes Scott College.

The New York Times has described Decatur as the "Brooklyn of Atlanta," and resident Catherine Lee agrees. *"The biggest way it's like Brooklyn is the neighborhood feel—you walk around the streets and you know people,"* said Lee, Decatur's downtown development manager who started a fashion and travel blog with her twin sister called Asian Cajuns. *"The local shops and restaurants are very Brooklyn-like."* Her favorite restaurant is Kimball House, a favorite Happy Hour destination for its raw oysters and martinis.

Lee's coworker, Linda Harris, a Decatur native and executive director of the Decatur Tourism Bureau, recalled how quiet Decatur was 20 years ago. *"We started doing festivals and events, thinking of the square as the community living room,"* she recalled. *"People were comfortable coming here and economic development followed. There's always something going on."*

The enclave today hosts three dozen festivals a year—including the AJC Decatur Book Festival, the nation's largest independent book festival, and the Decatur Arts Festival, a free event held every May featuring arts and live music. Harris said one venue, Eddie's Attic, put Decatur on the map. *"They bring all kinds of acoustic music and people like the Indigo Girls, John Mayer, and Sugarland all started here,"* she said.

Dan Whisenhunt, editor of local online news site, *Decaturish,* considers Decatur's density and walkability its most standout feature. *"It's kind of hard to find that in Atlanta—we have a well-developed downtown and sidewalks connecting pretty much every resident. Decatur also has three MARTA stations, so this is a very transit, multi-modal type of place."*

Druid Hills

Druid Hills was established as an Atlanta neighborhood in 1908 after prominent businessman Joel Hurt sold his Druid Hills project and Olmsted plan to the Druid Hills Corporation. The community is located inside the Perimeter four-and-a-half miles northeast of Atlanta.

Druid Hills residents enjoy amazing green space, including Olmsted Linear Park and Lullwater Conservation Garden, a woodland park and bird sanctuary. They also have easy access to many of Atlanta's most popular intown venues from nearby Little Five Points to Candler Park to the south and Decatur and Inman Park to the west. A three-bedroom home starts at $310,000 here, while a five-bedroom property is priced as high as $3.4 million.

Druid Hills was built around Olmsted Linear Park.
Pictured above is Deepdene, an old growth forest.
Credit: Marc Del Santro

Key employers include both Emory University and CDC. Fernbank Museum of Natural History is expanding its outdoor presence in the natural woodlands adjacent to the Museum, with new tree pods, highline trails, an education pavilion and a boardwalk.

"We've seen incredible growth in the access to things we can do in the last ten years," said Michelle Walldorff, constituent services coordinator for the DeKalb County Commissioner in Super District Six and a Druid Hills resident since 1994.

From the beginning, the neighborhood was designed around Olmsted Linear Park, named for its creator Frederick Law Olmsted, Sr., the nation's preeminent designer of parks and public open spaces, including Central Park in New York City.

All six park segments extend two miles along both sides of Ponce de Leon Avenue. Deepdene, the largest segment, features an old growth forest and a stream winding through its twenty-two acres.

"We have one tree in Deepdene that dates back to the Revolutionary War," said Sandy Kruger, a native Atlantan and the executive director of the Olmsted Linear Park Alliance (OLPA). The Alliance was born in the aftermath of Druid Hills residents taking up the community road fight to keep a super highway from being built through historic neighborhoods. Since then, the Alliance was established as a private-

public partnership and has raised over $10 million to rehabilitate and restore the park.

"We're here to preserve this historic landmark and educate the community about its significance not only to Druids Hills but also to other projects in the city… we want to have natural green spaces that are healthy and vibrant and are good for the community," she said.

Druid Hills native Walter Kellar, a project manager, couldn't agree more. He now lives in the 1930s home he grew up in a block-and-a-half from Fernbank. Deepdene was a favorite place for him to explore as a child. *"Our Boy Scout troop would camp out in the woods. We'd build treehouses in there, explore the creek and chase bugs—kind of like a Huckleberry Finn existence in the city that you normally wouldn't have in the suburbs,"* recalled Kellar, who returned to Atlanta in 1984 after studying on the West Coast and working in Germany and Canada.

"The best thing about Druid Hills is the green space and having a science museum like Fernbank nearby—also the fact that it's really close to a small town like Decatur with places to eat and things to do, whether it's recreational or business," he added.

East Atlanta Village

**Flatiron Restaurant & Bar in East Atlanta Village.
Credit: S. Sargent**

East Atlanta Village (EAV), a mile south of Little Five Points on Moreland Avenue or three miles east of downtown on I-20, is *"the best kept secret in Atlanta,"* according to *The Washington Post* and *"the epitome of cool and a neighborhood's neighborhood,"* according to *Creative Loafing*. A three-bedroom home is available for as low as $229,000, while a five-bedroom runs as high as $325,000.

EAV was the site of significant fighting during the Battle of Atlanta in July 1864. Today, many historic markers dot the neighborhood, including two upturned cannon at the spots where Confederate General Walker and Union General McPherson were killed. The neighborhood commemorates the area's role during its annual Battle of Atlanta Festival.

After the Civil War, East Atlanta recovered quickly, developing into an unincorporated town and Atlanta suburb. Moreland Avenue was little more than a dirt path along the county line, while Flat Shoals and Glenwood Avenues were the major highways that brought the farmers and their goods to town. East Atlanta was annexed by the City of Atlanta in 1909.

Dan Schaefer, a sound designer/engineer and owner of his own audio production firm, The SoundNut, moved to East Atlanta in late 1998 from Marietta. He missed the intown area, having previously lived in Castleberry Hill and Howell Station neighborhoods. *"I wanted to be intown and close to work. Looking at different neighborhoods, I could get a much better deal on a house in EAV back then,"* said Schaefer, describing his neighbors as *"very close-knit and diverse,"* with motorcycle mechanics and attorneys hanging out at various village establishments.

"The neighborhood is still very diverse," he said, noting that today he sees a lot more families.

Live music keeps the Village hopping every night of the week. People enjoy live DJs, pool and foosball, underground and foreign film, and shopping. *"There's something for everyone. If you want to go upscale, there's a place called the Argosy,"* said Schaefer, a drummer and member of the Atlanta-Decatur Dart Association. EAV bars are active in the

Association. Teams meet on Monday nights and play every team in the division twice, taking turns hosting the competition, Schaefer said.

Popular bars include the Elder Tree, Midway Pub, the Flatiron, The Glenwood, and The Earl ('East Atlanta Restaurant & Lounge'). *"It's a divey kind of place that has become a very popular music venue. They offer live music in the back, with a separate cover charge,"* noted Schaefer.

The annual neighborhood festival, the East Atlanta Strut, features a parade, often with residents dressing up their dogs, said Schaefer. The event includes an artists' market, children's events, live bands, and food. The Strut benefits local charities. More recently, the Village has added Notoberfest (the East Atlanta Beer Festival) and the Brownwood Park Bike Rally.

Brownwood Park, with its newly-renovated recreation center and computer lab, is located in the middle of the neighborhood.

Grant Park

Grant Park Mothball revelers celebrate, speakeasy-style!
Credit: Grant Park Neighborhood Association

This Victorian neighborhood has both a local and national historical designation. It is home to the oldest city park in Atlanta as well as host to an annual candlelight tour of homes in the fall and a tour of homes in the spring. Grant Park also is a popular enclave for the LGBT community, students, and young families, said Grant Park Neighborhood Association President Lauren Rocereta, who has lived in the neighborhood for ten years.

"Because of our historical designation, our home values stayed high even in the economic downturn," she said. *"When one house goes on the market here in Grant Park, it's off the market within a week, sometimes in a matter of days."*

Grant Park residents have diverse backgrounds, ages and income levels. Rocereta worries that as rent prices increase, Grant Park may no longer be in the affordability range of lower income groups, including students from nearby Georgia State University. *"We really want the diversity here to stay,"* she said. Housing prices on the low-end are $140,000, while some four-bedroom homes are priced as a high as $880,000.

The school cluster has gone through a renaissance as many of the professional young married couples who started families have opted to remain in Grant Park. Initially, the neighborhood helped start a charter elementary and middle school, and as more people have moved in, they have enthusiastically supported the public schools.

To fight property crime, the community relies on security patrols and off-duty police officers. *"A lot of the crime that used to hit us has affected neighborhoods around us more,"* Rocereta said.

A major event every fall is the Mothball, which began as a thank you to the tour of home volunteers and quickly became a neighborhood party.

Inman Park

Popular Inman Park destination Barcelona's was named *Creative Loafing's* Best Wine List and Best Spanish/Tapas for 2015.
Credit: Jeff Herr

The first planned residential suburb and first electric trolley neighborhood situated along the old rail corridors has become so much more. Located two miles east of downtown Atlanta, Inman Park adopted historical zoning in the early 2000s, which allowed the neighborhood to preserve its historic houses and provided guidelines for new construction. Inman Park today is a dynamic locale with walkable streets and hip bars and restaurants. The symbol of the neighborhood is a butterfly—for rebirth—with a face in each wing: one looking backward to the past and one looking forward into the future.

Redevelopment of industrial areas along the railroad corridor—the soon-to-be Beltline—resulted in mixed use projects that have created condos, apartments, restaurants, shops and services.

"*The real estate market in Inman Park is quite healthy, with listings selling quickly,*" said Pat Westrick, realtor with The Pat & Melissa Group, Re/Max Metro Atlanta Cityside.

In the last decade, the community of 1,500 mostly single-family homes has doubled, with two-thirds of its 3,000 residences now identified as multi-family, said Dennis Mobley, president of the Inman Park Neighborhood Association (IPNA).

"Inman Park has become a destination for dining out and maybe you will see somebody from 'The Vampire Diaries' or 'The Walking Dead,'" said Mobley, who moved into one of the neighborhood's century-old bungalows in 1997 with his wife. Two popular destinations are the Spanish tapas wine bar, Barcelona, and the Krog Street Market.

Westrick noted that single-family house prices in 2015 ranged from $1.3 million for a renovated vintage home to $310,000 for a small bungalow, which was ready for a re-do. Condo prices range from $145,000 for a two-bedroom one bath conversion to $773,000 for a new four-bedroom, 4-1/2 bath townhome.

"The diverse housing sizes in Inman Park, along with the many older apartment buildings, in-law suites and carriage house apartments, result in a great diversity of population: professionals, artists, students, wait-staff, entrepreneurs and retirees," Westrick said, adding, *"It makes for an interesting, eclectic neighborhood where neighbors are judged by how much they love the neighborhood, not by how much money they make or what they do."*

For Mobley, the best part of living in Inman Park is the *"activism of the neighborhood,"* which emerged during the road wars of the 70s, 80s, and 90s, when residents successfully fought the push to build freeways through the heart of Atlanta's intown neighborhoods.

"I tell people that the local activism of yesteryear morphed into what is today's Inman Park Festival and Tour of Homes."

Held the last weekend of April, the event draws tens of thousands of people to the neighborhood. According to Westrick, it began forty-five years ago *"as a way to demonstrate to banks, insurance companies and the media that the run-down and forgotten intown neighborhoods were attracting young, energetic homeowners who were fixing up old houses and establishing a sense of community that was worth investing in."*

Historic South Atlanta

The wall mural marking Historical South Atlanta's neighborhood.

Located a mile south of Turner Field and a mile north of Aaron's [Lakewood] Amphitheatre, Historic South Atlanta was formed in post-Civil War Atlanta as one of the first African-American neighborhoods that attracted teachers looking to educate the newly freed slaves and their children. The Freedmen's Aid Society helped establish Clark University, which moved into 450 acres south of Henderson's Crossing in 1883. A year later, a theological department was established that became Gammon Theological Seminary.

For over fifty years, Clark and Gammon were vital to the South Atlanta neighborhood until 1941 when Clark Atlanta relocated to southwest Atlanta—in a move to share resources with other historic black colleges. Street signs in the neighborhood still bear the names of former presidents and professors of Clark University and Gammon Theological Seminary.

Homes in the neighborhood start as low as $20,000 for a two-bedroom house and go as high as $125,000 for a three-bedroom property. Today, Historic South Atlanta has a strong neighborhood association and a unique partnership with a non-profit Christian-based organization, Focused Community Strategies, which operates three neighborhood businesses. The first business, Community Grounds, opened in 2010 and serves up both espresso and free Wi-Fi to residents. South Atlanta Bike Shop followed soon after, offering a way for young people to work and earn credit in the store to buy bikes or accessories to keep their bikes running. In May 2015, Carver Neighborhood Market opened, selling a variety of fresh produce and other items to residents who before had to take MARTA to get to the nearest grocery.

"Our hope is to have a neighborhood that's affordable and safe for all," said Jeff Delp, director of economic development for Focused Community Strategies. Delp, who enjoys a four-block walk to work every day, moved to the neighborhood 15 years ago from Philadelphia. *"Something special has been created here—it's been a long time coming and it's been hard work. Not a lot of folks know about us and sometimes that's good. It's a small town in a big city,"* he said.

Delp's neighbor, Andrej Ciho, came to the neighborhood in 2009 and started the bike shop a year later. The Michigan native said that over the last five years, 160 kids have earned bikes through the economic development program, with some earning enough to get bikes for siblings and other relatives. *"Our neighbors depend on bicycles to get to and from work and school—so this is a very tangible way to help our neighbors provide for themselves because of the transportation challenges here,"* said Ciho. The program's impact goes well beyond the bikes in helping prepare teens to be responsible young adults. Several have gone on to college.

Jeff Delp and Latia Holmes inside Carver Neighborhood Market.

Intown Southwest – Oakland City, Ft. McPherson, Adair Park and Sylvan Hills

Many expect the next Atlanta area to see dramatic growth and development is in the historic neighborhoods around Ft. McPherson, site of the new Tyler Perry Studios. The main communities include Oakland City (including Murphy's Crossing), Adair Park, and Sylvan Hills. Adair Park already has seen a lot of real estate activity, as has Murphy's Crossing, with its proximity to the Atlanta Beltline. Properties in the area range in price from $70,000 for a three-bedroom house to $497,000 for a three-bedroom home or $180,000 for a two-bedroom condo.

"Murphy's Crossing is already being inhabited by artists—that's a sign that things are changing there," said Bill de St. Aubin, CEO of Sizemore Group, the architectural planning firm that is reimagining how to redevelop 147 acres in Ft. McPherson retained by the city. The Group projects that eighty new homes in the area will be occupied for renovation or adaptive reuse in the next five years. As for the area around Ft. McPherson, plans are in the works to build a community theatre that will be owned by Perry but will be open for public use, too.

Oakland City's new playground and neighborhood pool.
Credit: Amy Johnson

"We believe Ft. McPherson will become a combination of retail, townhomes, and apartments and it will have a little historic district, too. The project has the potential to be a movie town and have places that show up in Tyler Perry's movies similar to how the BlueBird Café is now a recognized place in Nashville," said de St. Aubin of an existing venue made more famous as a key location in the ABC drama "Nashville."

Oakland City, which borders Ft. McPherson to the south, already has a Hollywood claim to fame—the house of grandma Medea, who Perry plays in several of his movies. Oakland City has two other assets—it is right on the Atlanta Beltline and has a MARTA station, according to de St. Aubin. Already developers are submitting proposals to redevelop part of the Oakland City MARTA station parking lot into condos and a mixed-use development.

Amy Johnson, a registered storyteller and 25-year resident of Oakland City, expressed excitement for the coming of the studios and what it will mean for her neighbors.

"The energy around all the potential development is really important for us right now. We're feeling it, loving it, and doing what we can to support it," she said.

Historically, Oakland City was its own city from 1894 until 1910 when it was annexed by the city of Atlanta. The community of 1,400 homes is located a mile north of the former base.

Eight neighborhoods, including Sylvan Hills and Adair Park, have come together under the name Intown Southwest, and are working together to give tours to potential investors and show support to existing businesses, indicated Johnson, adding that Atlanta Technical College in Sylvan Hills is looking to bring in a technical program tied to the film industry. It already has one film course, Intro to Video Production, and is offering a special workshop in 2016, with more courses to follow.

"Those 147 acres hold a lot of promise and we are not ignoring that," Johnson said.

Little Five Points

This tiny eclectic and edgy business district two-and-a-half miles east of downtown and easily accessible by I-20 is often described as Atlanta's "hippie hood." Little Five Points (L5P), known for its counter-culture appeal, attracts young singles and families to nearby Candler Park on its east and Inman Park on its west. The highest sale price in 2015 in Candler Park was $1.07 million for a four-bedroom, 3 ½ bath home; the least expensive condo was $72,000, with a one-bedroom/one bath.

L5P considers itself the Atlanta version of Manhattan's Greenwich Village and New Orleans' French Quarter.

The Vortex in Little Five Points.
Credit: Colin Murphy/The Vortex Bar & Grill

"It's always been very accepting of all types of people," noted Pam Majors, owner of the iconic Junkman's Daughter, who has lived in the area since 1976 (her home is a few blocks away in Candler Park).

"By 1978-1979, L5P become pro-neighborhood," added early property owner Don Bender, who rallied groups to buy properties in the neighborhood and described the first L5P residents as locals who were *"politically and social-movement active." "We polled resources."* Bender opened the L5P Pub and it became a gathering place.

Majors recalled that artists and students began moving into Little Five from Virginia-Highland to find more affordable housing. At the time, many storefronts were empty. *"People started opening up little stores and things just spread from there,"* recalled Majors.

Some of the first shops to open their doors included Sevananda Natural Foods Market, Abbadabba's, and the veteran music shop, Wax 'n Facts. L5P has built a reputation for having some of the best music stores in the city that offer rare and vintage recordings. As a result, it's attracted music enthusiasts and collectors from all over the world.

Credit: Junkman's Daughter

Majors said she started her shop in 1982 after her parents retired. *"I had to close their store down. They had a salvage business and had bought out stores for forty years. I literally am a junkman's daughter,"* she said, with a laugh. She found a 1,000-square-foot space and opened a store on Euclid Avenue, later moving to its current location on Moreland Avenue. Between 1982 and 1994, the store grew to 10,000 square feet.

"We try to be really funky. We were the first people to bring in Doc Martens to the Southeast and the only place to go for colored hair dye," Majors said. *"People would come from all the adjoining states on the weekends to shop here."*

Bender is the chairman of the board of the L5P Community Investment District, which was formed a little over a year ago. He said he would like to see the arts be a stronger component of L5P, noting that there already are three theaters in the neighborhood: Variety Playhouse, 7 Stages Theatre, and Horizon Theatre Company.

"We want to build a parking deck behind the theatres to make them more viable," Bender said. *"That would lead to stronger eateries."*

A major push right now is to make Moreland Avenue more pedestrian-friendly. *"It was widened back in the 1980s when the city was looking to create a highway,"* Bender said. *"We want to decrease it by a lane and put bike lanes on either side. That improvement is funded and will be coming in the next couple of years,"* he added.

To Majors, all the quirky, independently owned little shops are the real draw to the neighborhood today.

A popular hangout next door to the Junkman's Daughter is The Vortex Bar & Grill, which was opened by three siblings who relocated to Atlanta from southern California back in 1991. This 21-and-older bar is easily identified by its massive skull entrance-way, which was inspired by the roadside attractions owner Michael Benoit remembered from his childhood out west. The Vortex also operates the Laughing Skull Comedy Club in the rear of its Midtown location.

Other cool bars popular with singles include the Star Community Bar, the Porter Beer Bar, Wrecking Bar Brewpub, and The Euclid Avenue Yacht Club. And, residents won't want to miss the annual Little 5 Points Halloween Festival and Parade.

Midtown

Two out of three Midtown residents are now millennials.
Credit: Midtown Alliance

Midtown, situated between Buckhead and downtown Atlanta, is the second-largest business district in Atlanta.

"What makes Midtown unique is the fact that it's a true live, work, play walkable urban district. There are very few of those in Atlanta and in the Southeast," said Kevin Green, president & CEO of Midtown Alliance.

Green said $5 billion has been invested in Midtown in the last fifteen years. *"We are currently seeing sixteen high-rise construction projects right now within one square-mile area,"* he added.

Properties range in price from $80,000 for a one-bedroom condo, to $2.3 million for a three-bedroom condo in the heart of Midtown.

Midtown was designed to promote walking—everyone is within a six-minute stroll from one of four MARTA rail lines. It's also an area that has the largest concentration of arts and culture in the Southeast as well as being adjacent to Piedmont Park, Atlanta's "Central Park." Residents are within an easy walk to the Atlanta Beltline Eastside trail and the Atlanta Botanical Gardens.

Georgia Tech's campus is in the heart of Midtown.
Credit: Rob Felt/Georgia Institute of Technology

"All of that makes the area really unique but when you couple that with the economic engines that are within Midtown that include Georgia Tech, Emory Hospital Midtown, and the Savannah College of Art and Design, all within this live-work-play community, Midtown has created an ecosystem that is second to none," according to Green.

Home to Georgia Tech, Midtown now accounts for 70% of all tech jobs in Atlanta. About 65,000 people work in the district.

"Companies are locating where they think they can attract and retain the talent and to get the talent; it's about quality of place and creating a superior experience for people," said Green, noting that Georgia Tech has become a "center of gravity" for companies looking to tap into their talent pool.

Georgia Tech made the smart decision to locate in the middle of Midtown, creating the "Technology Square" innovation district in 2003 and featuring a hotel, classrooms, and retail space. It also houses Georgia Tech's Advanced Technology Development Center, the oldest and largest university-based incubator in the United States, Georgia Tech VentureLab, the number-two ranked incubator in the world, and its Flashpoint accelerator program for technology startups.

"At least a dozen corporations have set up innovation centers within Technology Square," said Green. *"We are seeing a lot of start-ups and co-working spaces. In addition to that you're going to have the global headquarters of NCR next to Technology Square."*

NCR expects to bring 3,600 jobs to Midtown once its headquarters is built at the corner of Spring Street and 8th Street. Kaiser Permanente is establishing a $20 million information technology campus in Midtown—a project that will create about 900 jobs and reaffirms Atlanta's status as a health-care IT industry cluster. Other tech firms newly established in Midtown include Sage Software and secure payment processor, Worldpay.

With all the exciting growth in Midtown, it's no surprise that many young people are choosing this area to build their careers. Two out of three Midtown residents are millennials, including Shelbi Havenga, an office manager for NCR Corporation's Midtown office.

"The walkability is what I love about Midtown—being able to go to amazing lunch places and after work there are so many options for getting a drink with colleagues. The Fox is just down the street, if you want to go to a play or a concert," said Havenga, a Georgia State University grad who has worked at NCR for a year.

She considers Midtown's vibe more "fast-paced, with an exciting nightlife" compared with the laid-back feel of other intown neighborhoods. Her favorite places include the Vortex's Midtown location with its comedy club and Shakespeare Tavern. She also likes West Midtown's Ormsby's, a stylish speakeasy with craft beers and pub fare, bocce, shuffleboard, darts, and pool tables.

Other popular venues are the Center Stage Theater, which offers three different performance areas, and the iconic Fox Theatre. The Atlanta Symphony Orchestra and the Alliance Theater are also mainstays.

"You can't get bored here. There's always something to do—something to discover," Havenga said. *"I think Midtown is one of the hottest places to be in Atlanta."*

Old Fourth Ward

Old Fourth Ward Park.
Credit: Anne Wainscott-Sargent

This historic enclave where Martin Luther King, Jr. grew up is now a thriving intown neighborhood, with the Beltline running through it. The O4W district is known for lofts, markets (including the Ponce City Market housed in the former Sears, Roebuck & Company building), and artistic expression sketched and painted everywhere—under bridges, on the sides of warehouses converted into trendy restaurants, and even on light poles.

Residents are drawn to the O4W for its diversity and demographics, which embrace a vision of inclusiveness and a caring community that is "connected"—mirroring the purpose of the Beltline to connect neighborhoods.

Credit: Sarah Dorio

"O4W is an incredible success story—the spirit of public art embraced during the renaissance era is alive here," said painter and social worker Callahan McDonough, a 35-year intown resident who was drawn to this historic neighborhood a decade ago as an empty nester looking for a more artsy place with a creative edge to live. She got it and more, becoming one of the first to buy a unit in the trendy Sager Lofts, a short walk to the Beltline and Ponce City Market.

Old Fourth Ward's highest sales price in 2015 was $718,000 for a four-bedroom, three-and-a-half bath home; its lowest was $47,000 for a one-bedroom, one-bath condo.

June draws Atlantans from all over to the District to enjoy events such as the Atlanta Cycling Festival / Beltline Tour, the Atlanta Summer Beer Fest at Masquerade, and the two-day Old Fourth Ward Arts Festival at the Historic Fourth Ward Park.

Vinings

**Vinings Jubilee with a distant view of Midtown and Downtown Atlanta.
Credit: Phlinda Schumacher**

Located alongside the Chattahoochee River ten miles northwest of downtown Atlanta, Vinings also borders the new Atlanta Braves stadium scheduled to open in 2017. It earned its official name in the 1840s when the area became a construction stop on the Western and Atlantic Railroad. The principal architect at this stop was William H. Vining who was there to construct a railroad bridge. During this time, numerous supplies were sent to "Vining's station" and soon the Vinings name was adopted.

Home to over 9,600 residents and 1,700 businesses, Vinings is an unincorporated town that was originally known as Crossroads and later as Paces in 1830. The neighborhood offers residents many diversions, including outdoor festivals, parades, concerts, and farmer's markets. Housing prices range from $75,000 for a two-bedroom condo to $3 million for a four-bedroom home.

Fashionable boutiques, restaurants, and specialty stores are nestled in the lush and historic Vinings Village. More than 35% of the city's businesses have paid employees (versus being solo entrepreneurs), contributing to Vinings' unemployment rate of 2.5%. A major employer is Home Depot.

Donald Hawkins, publisher of *Vinings Lifestyle*, a consumer-oriented magazine he began in September 2015, observed that people from not only Vinings proper but also surrounding communities of Smyrna, Mableton, and even Austell identify themselves as residents of this charming enclave.

"Because the area is so small, it makes it a very unique place to live because of how close the businesses are to the community. It feels like an area like [the TV sitcom] "Cheers," where you walk into a restaurant, and see the owner sitting at the bar having a pint with a local. They learn your name and you know theirs," said Hawkins.

A building in Vinings Jubilee with the gleaming Overlook III corporate office building behind. Credit: Phlinda Schumacher

The price point for housing in Vinings is rising, said Hawkins, noting that *"the Braves coming here has changed everything."* A new mixed-use development is underway, as well as four new office towers, several new restaurants, and a new Omni Hotel NW—all driven by SunTrust Park, future home of the new Atlanta Braves stadium at the intersection of I-285 and I-75.

Other area highlights include: Cumberland Mall, Cobb Galleria, Cobb Energy Performing Arts Centre, Chattahoochee River National Recreation Area, Vinings Historic Preservation Society, Historic Pace

House & Pavilion, Vinings Jubilee, Silver Comet Trail, and Heritage Park.

Hawkins said signs of new development are evident everywhere, even in buildings previously dormant. *"People are excited. The area has been progressively growing anyway, but now that there are so many things coming, you are starting to find a lot more people getting involved. One illustration of Vinings being so cool is evident by the fact that we've been able to grow into a 60-page magazine in four months. It's just an exciting time to be in Vinings,"* he said.

Virginia-Highland

Established around the turn of the century, Virginia-Highland is one of Atlanta's oldest and most popular intown neighborhoods. Known by many locals as 'VaHi', the neighborhood of 9,247 residents gets its formal name from the intersection of Virginia and N. Highland Avenues, which is at the center of the community's main business node.

"People are amazed by how walkable the community is—it's all tree-lined streets and sidewalks," said John Becker, a former board member for the VaHi Civic Association (VHCA), who lived in the neighborhood for 15 years. *"The neighborhood works closely with Trees Atlanta to maintain the tree canopy with annual plantings."*

Becker said that VaHi is an intown neighborhood with *"a small town feel,"* yet is extremely close to downtown Atlanta. *"It's a very inclusive community."*

Residents enjoy an inventory of unique historic bungalow and cottage-style homes, as well as a number of older apartment buildings. Pricing for a one-bedroom condo is as low as $85,000, while some five-bedroom homes are on the market for $1.4 million. Piedmont Park, Atlanta's crown jewel of green space, forms the southwest border of the neighborhood near Monroe Drive. The Callanwolde Fine Arts Center—where many residents enjoy taking photography or art classes—is on Briarcliff Road along the neighborhood's east side.

"*VaHi, Inman Park, Poncey-Highland, and Old Fourth Ward are all extremely fortunate that the Eastside Trail was the first two-mile stretch of the Atlanta Beltline to be completed,*" added Becker, who recently bought a condo along the trail, which is located just to the west of VaHi.

Becker said that residents live close to local businesses, ranging from shops to restaurants to popular nightlife destinations. The neighborhood also has three public parks and nearby access to some of the city's finest public and private schools.

Many residents are active in neighborhood organizations, a parent's organization, a neighborhood watch program, and an after-hours security patrol. The community's two major fundraising events are Summerfest in June and a Tour of Homes in December.

On the eve of Summerfest neighbors gather for dinner and movie at John Howell Park.
Credit: John Becker

Becker, who serves as co-chair for Summerfest, noted that the entire neighborhood opens up to enjoy the festivities. "*Everyone is having parties on their porch. On Friday afternoon we have a residents-only parade and a catered community dinner in John Howell Park followed by a movie that night for the kids.*"

Like all intown neighborhoods, VaHi struggles with traffic problems and parking. Non-residents coming to VaHi will find a lot of metered parking that is strictly enforced.

"More parking comes with a cost, though," Becker added. *"As the city continues to evolve and we live closer to our offices and other important destinations, we'll likely find ourselves out of our cars more and on our bikes or using public transportation."*

Historic West End

**Wren's Nest in Historic West End.
Credit: Jonathan Hillyer**

Historic West End, Atlanta's "oldest suburb," is located just south of downtown and I-20. It was settled in 1835, and the original name of the West End was Whitehall (after the White Hall Inn). It was renamed in 1867 after London's theatre district and served as the stagecoach shop, tavern, post office, and home of the 503rd Militia district, as well as the election precinct.

West End officially became a part of Atlanta on January 1, 1894. It was the first locally designated historic district in the city. Today, this predominantly African-American urban neighborhood and first Beltline community offers affordable single-family homes.

Brent Brewer, an engineer and Georgia Tech grad, moved to the West End in 2003, after buying a 1920s era Craftsman bungalow to refurbish. He said that many of his neighbors bonded over the shared experience of renovating their homes. *"What we say is people come into the neighborhood for the particular house that they fell in love with, but we keep them here by being extra neighborly,"* he explained. Newer residents now are buying completely renovated homes that sell for upwards of $200,000, he added.

While home vacancy and absentee homeowners remain a challenge, the West End's historic designation has helped. Residents enjoy two museums—the historic Wren's Nest, which features a museum, a storytelling program, and an amphitheater that Brewer described as the 'Chastain of the Southwest' (referring to the popular music venue, Chastain Park Amphitheater) and the Hammonds House and Museum, which features 19th-century antiques and a notable collection of African-American art.

"West End's rich cultural history, beautiful architecture, and refreshing street grid make for easy discovery and exploration," said Lain Shakespeare, a descendent of Wren's Nest founder Joel Chandler Harris, who served as executive director of the historic home from June 2006 until October 2011.

He considers Wren's Nest, along with the Shrine of the Black Madonna and Hammonds House, *"cultural anchors of the neighborhood."*

"As a National Historic Landmark, Wren's Nest will always represent West End's cultural and architectural history. As an organization, it will strive to represent the creativity of the students and storytellers of the neighborhood."

Shakespeare started the Scribes Program at KIPP STRIVE and at Brown Middle School—programs he said are enabling *"the students around us to become great storytellers who can communicate more effectively and vividly in life and in their careers."*

"There are a ton of activities to get people out of their house and create community," added Brewer, citing the annual candlelight concert held at the Wren's Nest Amphitheater every May as a fundraiser for the neighborhood. For the last two years, the West End has hosted the Atlanta Streets Alive event in the spring. The neighborhood closes its streets to cars and throws a party on a Sunday afternoon.

"People who move here call West End an Atlanta Streets Alive neighborhood—that means bike-friendly, walkable, with access to mass transit, and affordable," Brewer said.

Key Communities outside the Perimeter

Alpharetta

Alpharetta, located twenty miles northeast of Atlanta, was incorporated on December 11, 1858, becoming the county seat of the newly formed Milton County. The territory comprising Milton County had once been a part of the Cherokee Nation. Alpharetta's economy was cotton-based for decades. Farmers grew cotton and downtown businesses opened to seed, fertilize, process, sell, and ship the product. In 1901, the Webb Guano Warehouse opened for business in the landmark Cotton House building on Milton Avenue. At various times three gins operated in Alpharetta.

Today, Alpharetta is the sixth-fastest growing city in the United States, according to the 2012 U.S. Census, with more than 62,000 residents. Housing runs as low as $125,000 for a three-bedroom house to $6.2 million for a 10-bedroom estate home. Condo living starts at $92,000 for a one-bedroom and can go as high as $1.4 million for a condo with five bedrooms.

Known as the "Technology City of the South," Alpharetta is home to six hundred tech firms, including fifteen enterprise and co-location data centers. It was the first city in Georgia to offer gigabit internet speeds (more than one hundred times faster than typical broadband connections), rolling out the high-speed service in Avalon, the city's new mixed-use development that opened in October 2014 and is now in its second phase of construction.

Samir Abdullahi, economic development manager for the city, said one interesting facet to Alpharetta is that it has twenty million square feet of office space. *"Buckhead has twenty-one million square feet, so we have quite a sizeable office market that you don't find in a suburban community."*

ADP, McKesson, Verizon Wireless, Lexis/Nexis, Comcast, and UPS are the top employers. Alpharetta was recently named the Best Small City to Start a Business by Entrepreneur.com and the Best Atlanta Suburb by Movoto.

Abdullahi explained that Alpharetta's City Center project is building on the concept of Avalon. It's focused on creating a sense of "place" within the downtown so all these workers don't just leave at the end of their work day.

The back of City Center will encompass City Hall, the large park behind it, and the future Fulton County Library, while the front will include new development.

"There will be 32,000 square feet of office space, seven new restaurants, and 100 high-end luxury apartments with first floor restaurant and retail space," Abdullahi said.

Developers closed on land buys in January 2016, with construction starting in April, and it will take eighteen to twenty-four months to complete.

Already community events are being oriented more toward downtown, from the annual Christmas Tree Lighting ceremony to Taste of Alpharetta, a dining festival held every May that attracts over 50,000 festival-goers. The festival used to be held in Wills Park but now is based downtown, noted Abdullahi. The Alpharetta Arts StreetFest, held during the three-day Memorial Day weekend, features nearly 100 artists, musicians, and performers who fill the streets of historic downtown.

Every Saturday morning from April through October, residents enjoy the Alpharetta Farmers Market, where they can buy locally grown produce, grass-fed meats, cheese, baked goods, and more. Thursday evenings in the spring and fall brings Alpharetta Food Truck Alley, an opportunity for the community to eat outside, stroll downtown streets, and listen to good music.

Michel Guilet, director of product management for Juice Analytics, a ten-year-old data visualization and data presentation company, works in the recently opened ATC Innovation Center alongside other tech firms, including startups. *"We build better products when we learn from others around us and the community. We're so much sharper participating in a community of peers,"* he said of the benefit of being co-located with other tech innovators.

When he and his wife Natalie moved to Alpharetta fourteen years ago, the city's growth was already evident with the new NorthPoint Mall. The couple has two children and wanted to raise their family in a place with great schools and diversity. Alpharetta has some of the top schools in Georgia and boasts a beautiful greenway system along Big Creek. Two major parks are Webb Bridge and Wills Parks, with the latter featuring a leading equestrian facility.

"For us, our kids walk to their elementary school, and the park we like is within walking distance. Across the street is the library. I think convenience and Alpharetta's family friendliness are major draws for us," he said, adding that they have seen more diversity with the number of Vietnamese, Chinese, Korean, Indian, and Russian families making Alpharetta home. *"I think that's due to some degree to the tech community here,"* he said.

Marietta

The historic Marietta Square serves as a park and traditional city center.
Credit: Marietta Visitors Bureau

Located fifteen miles northwest of Atlanta, Marietta serves as the Cobb County seat and has a population of 56,579. Marietta offers Atlantans several fun destinations, including the historic Marietta Square, with its shops and dining. Another must-see nearby venue is Kennesaw Mountain National Battlefield Park.

CNNMoney.com named Marietta one of the top 25 places in the United States to retire in 2011. Marietta's biggest employers include Cobb County Schools, WellStar Health System, and Lockheed Martin, according to the Cobb County Office of Economic Development.

Incorporated in 1834, Marietta went from being a farming community to more industrial with the coming of the railroad in 1842. During the Civil War, both the Confederate and Union armies set up medical headquarters in Marietta, with many buildings converted into hospitals, explained Amy Reed, curator of Exhibits and Education at the Marietta Museum of History. During WWII, Bell Aircraft established a manufacturing plant leading to a major population boom. *"The number of residents tripled from 10,000 to 30,000 overnight,"* said Reed. In 1941, Dobbins Air Force was built and Lockheed Martin took over the Bell plant in 1951 to help supply aircraft during the Korean conflict.

"Marietta has an old-fashioned feel of a community," said lifelong resident Jan Galt, whose family had a furniture business in the Marietta Square from 1950 to 2001, and who lives in a 1940s-era home two blocks from the square. She noted that many of the bungalows and small homes of Bell and Lockheed workers are now being purchased and updated by young families. Housing prices vary from $49,000 for a two-bedroom condo to $700,000 for a three-bedroom unit, to as high as $9.1 million for a luxurious seven-bedroom estate home.

The community's original railroad tracks run through the Square. *"The Square is still the hub of the social life here. Within a four-block radius, we have six different museums (including the Gone with the Wind Museum) and three or four theaters, which do different types of shows from cabaret to improv to traditional holiday fare such as 'A Christmas Carol,'"* she added.

In the summer, Marietta hosts a Concert in the Park the last Friday night of the month from April through September and the Marietta Square Farmers Market goes from January through December, featuring Georgia-grown and made products.

Galt described Marietta Public Schools as "excellent," adding that several of her friends are school teachers. *"Marietta has a reputation for passionate teachers who really care about students. They also have good administrators. My oldest stepson credits the football coaches at Marietta High School for keeping him on the straight and narrow,"* she said. One of the city's more famous residents was Alice McLellan Birney, founder of the National PTA.

The Big Chicken, a Marietta icon.

The most well-known Marietta landmark is the Big Chicken, a towering steel structure with a moving beak and eyes that rises above a KFC restaurant at the intersection of Cobb Parkway and Roswell Road. Residents frequently reference where they live from their location to the Big Chicken, which has been a question on the game show, "Jeopardy," twice.

Norcross

Norcross, a diverse community and one of sixteen municipalities in Gwinnett County, was once known as Atlanta's "favorite summer resort." Incorporated in 1870 by Atlanta entrepreneur J.J. Thrasher, the railroad town is the second-oldest city in Gwinnett County and the first to be placed on the National Register of Historic Places. The Eastern Continental Divide runs through the heart of the original community, passing along Thrasher Park (established the year Norcross was established) and down the middle of North Peachtree Street.

"The location of Norcross is really incredible in that you can get just about anywhere you want to go—downtown, lakes, mountains—because of all the different roads here," said Norcross Mayor, Bucky Johnson, who moved to the community with his wife in 2003 after retiring as Georgia Tech's director of bands. *"My wife and I are both Atlanta natives and had lived all over metro area, but had never been to downtown Norcross until we were invited by friends to visit. It has a real small town, quaint, neighborly feel."*

Quaint definitely applies to Norcross's historic downtown, with its old brick buildings featuring restaurants and boutique shops. Railraod tracks run through the downtown center, which includes an historic park and a huge children's playground area. Concerts are held in the park every other summer weekend while the community center hosts a monthly Friday night concert.

Thrasher Park in Norcross draws kids because of the nearby train depot.

Johnson said three hundred events a year are held in the community, from a dizzying array of car shows to the annual Bluesberry Festival and BrewFest. His favorite events include the historic home tour the first weekend in December, where each home features unique music of the season, the Pre-Fourth of July celebration held on July 3rd downtown, and the annual Norcross ArtFest every October.

Norcross is also small—extending only 6.4 square miles (it was 75 square miles before nearby Peacthree Corners became its own city in 2011). Home to the Atlanta Braves' AAA team, Norcross is extremely business friendly: NerdWallet voted it among Georgia's top 10 places to launch a business.

"We've got 4,000 businesses in Norcross and probably only 2,500 single-family homes," said Johnson, adding that housing includes historic and modern homes priced from $50,000 on the lower end to over $1 million. Employers in warehousing and logistics dominate Norcross' business community. They include product packaging giant RockTenn, Hyundai Construction Equipment Americas, and a large FedEx automated distribution facility.

"Being in Gwinnett County you have access to great schools and fantastic parks," added Johnson, noting that the public school system has won the prestigious Broad Prize twice, tying in 2014 with a Florida school district. The award honors the best-performing urban school districts that also have reduced achievement gaps among low-income students and students of color.

"Norcross has a really small town feel but yet it's very metropolitan. There is a very active and engaged group of citizens who make it feel homey," he said, concluding, *"A good quality of life—that's what really draws people here and keeps them here."*

Peachtree City

**Residents deck out their golf carts for their 4th of July parade.
Credit: City of Peachtree City**

Located thirty-one miles from downtown Atlanta, and a short drive to nearby Fayette and Newnan, Peachtree City has amazing amenities, most notably ninety miles of golf cart paths. Established in 1959, the community features three lakes, two nature trails, three golf courses, and a 2,500-seat amphitheater. Many residents work for the airlines and large corporations, and more recently people from the film industry.

"Peachtree City started out as a planned community and it still is. Even though it has really grown, it still maintains its identity," noted Soumaya Khalifa, who lived in Peachtree City for twenty-six years. She and her husband, who works for a large Japanese firm, raised their three children there.

Khalifa started her own consulting company and a nonprofit, the Islamic Speakers Bureau of Atlanta, while living in Peachtree City. Her non-profit organized several interfaith projects in the community, including a summer program to feed the underprivileged. She said back when her family first moved to Peachtree City, it had only one grocery store. Now there are close to ten.

"Peachtree City is really wonderful in how quiet it is. It's a beautiful place to raise kids—very family-oriented," she said, explaining that the

biggest draw was the high-quality public school system. Homes are priced as low as $140,000 for a one-bedroom house to $3.5 million for a six-bedroom estate home. Condos range in price from $119,000 to $191,000.

Khalifa also likes the diversity in Peachtree City and Fayetteville. She said there are plenty of pockets of Atlanta that are welcoming to minority groups. *"We happen to be Muslim and when we moved there, we would drive to downtown Atlanta for the kids to go to weekend school. Now, there are three different mosques in the Fayette-Coweta county area."*

A favorite family activity was attending Peachtree City's 4th of July Parade, where residents would ride in their golf carts decked out in red, white and blue. The city, which has its own airport, also hosts the Great Georgia Air Show at Falcon Field in October.

"Peachtree City provided a great education for my children. It's like you're in a little city yet you have easy access to Atlanta. You get the best of both worlds," she said.

Roswell

Directional sign in Historic Roswell.

Roswell, located twenty-six miles north of downtown Atlanta, is the eighth-largest city in Georgia and has grown dramatically in the last 20 years.

City founder Roswell King saw the potential of the rushing waters at the joining of the Chattahoochee River with Vickery (Big) Creek. His Roswell Manufacturing Company, incorporated in 1839, included a mill to harness the power of the local rivers to make textiles. The well-planned town included a central square, mill village, church, and quaint stores. The layout and architecture was influenced by King's New England background.

Today, Roswell is known for its historical charm, its family-friendly neighborhoods, strong schools, and nationally recognized Recreation, Parks, Historic & Cultural Affairs Departments, a five-time finalist for the National Gold Medal Award for Excellence in Park and Recreation Management. Housing starts as low as $80,000 for a one-bedroom condo. A three-bedroom home can cost as little as $140,000, while a six-bedroom property costs as much as $5 million. The historic downtown, with its quaint restaurants and galleries, is a major draw for residents and visitors.

"Canton Street is probably one of the great historic main streets that took historic homes and made a whole district out of it. It never lost its historic charm; it always has that sense of place that goes back generations," said Roswell resident Bill De St. Aubin, whose company, Sizemore Group, does architectural planning and community design.

Roswell also was the first Georgia city to be named a bike-friendly community in 2006 by the League of American Bicyclists. *Frommer's* named Roswell one of the top three cities in the nation

Atlanta native Catherine Scully with her baby, Rachel, on Canton Street after house-hunting in Roswell.

to raise a family, while the city topped *Atlanta Magazine's* list of the best places to live in the Metro Atlanta area twice. Residents enjoy easy access to the Chattahoochee River, where several rowing leagues operate. In the summer and fall, residents take to the river on kayaks and tubes in what locals call "Shoot the Hooch."

"I live, work, and play in Roswell," said Dr. Charlie Weiss, a chiropractor and father of two who moved to the community in 1995. *"My family pretty much spends our summers at Roswell Area Park."*

Weiss said the city does a great job of providing family activities, whether it's concerts in the park, "dive-in" movies at the area pool or Alive after 5, held the third Thursday of each month beginning in April through October. A trolley takes residents up and down Canton Street to visit galleries, shop at the downtown shops and boutiques, and dine out at one of the trendy restaurants along Canton.

"I love how Roswell preserves its history," said twenty-six year Roswell resident Dianna Avena, a mother of three who operates Roswell Ghost Tour, a year-round walking tour operator that takes residents to the most haunted areas along the historic mill village. Roswell also offers daily tours and special events at three historical antebellum mansions: Archibald Smith Plantation Home, Bulloch Hall, and Barrington Hall.

The annual "Roswell Remembers" ceremony remains Georgia's largest Memorial Day ceremony, attracting 6,000 to 7,000 spectators. Youth Day every October began in 1950 when a group of parents sponsored a parade and a day of activities to honor Roswell's youth. Residents also enjoy wildlife programs, camps, and Halloween hikes at nearby Chattahoochee Nature Center.

Weiss said that Roswell's biggest challenges include traffic and how to maintain Roswell's historical identity as it tries to attract younger residents with walkable, mixed-use developments—a trend counter to Roswell's desire to protect neighborhoods from commercial zoning through buffering.

"Roswell continues to be a fantastic place to live. Residents are straightforward, helpful, caring. The people of Roswell are its biggest strength," Weiss said.

Sandy Springs

Sandy Springs has roughly 100,000 residents. It is among the top ten fastest-growing retirement communities in the country and also has the largest concentration of major healthcare facilities in metro Atlanta, including Northside Hospital, Saint Joseph's Hospital, and Children's Healthcare of Atlanta.

The community once was the site of a Cherokee and Creek Indian campsite and is named for the natural springs bubbling up through the clear white sand there. Accessible from both Georgia 400 and I-285, Sandy Springs is in the middle of the metro area's most popular attractions. A small portion of Sandy Springs extends inside the Perimeter to the Atlanta city limit. Most of this area is comfortably affluent and centers on scenic, mansion-filled single-lane roads such as Northside Drive, Mt. Paran Road, and Powers Ferry Road. The two last stops on MARTA's north line are in Sandy Springs.

**The iconic "King" and "Queen" office towers in Sandy Springs.
Credit: City of Sandy Springs**

More than 3,700 businesses call Sandy Springs home, including UPS, First Data, Newell Rubbermaid, and Intercontinental Exchange (parent to the New York Stock Exchange). Despite having more Fortune 500 corporations per capita than any other U.S. city, Sandy Springs' small businesses fuel most of the community's growth.

Jessica Gardner, owner of a music education business, Blueprint To Success, moved to Sandy Springs in 2009 for its affordability, safety, and proximity to Atlanta.

"It's quiet and you have great access to the Chattahoochee River and parks for walking trails," said Gardner.

Surrounded by more than 950 acres of parks and natural areas, Sandy Springs enjoys twenty-two miles of shoreline along the Chattahoochee River.

In the time she's lived in the area, Gardner said the city has grown dramatically. *"The population here has just exploded in the last few years,"* she said. The U.S. Census bureau noted that the population grew 16.3 percent from 2000 to 2013 alone.

"Interestingly, Sandy Springs has become a mecca for the quick-serve restaurant (QSR) industry too, with Arby's along with several other competing brands having their headquarters here," said Jason Rollins, manager, Corporate Communications, Arby's Restaurant Group, Inc. *"Similar to Detroit and the auto industry and High Point, N.C., and the furniture industry, the area has become somewhat known as the QSR capital of the U.S., primarily due to the central location, attractive economic climate, and close proximity to [the] airport."*

In addition to Arby's, Popeyes Louisiana Chicken, Moe's Southwest Grill (Focus Brands), Krystal, and Church's Chicken are all headquartered in the Perimeter area.

The annual Sandy Springs Festival, which celebrated its 30th year in September 2015, features a juried artist's market, civic and business expo, performances by regional acts and community bands, a children's area with crafts and activities, the annual Kiwanis Pet Parade, a 10K/5K race, a food court, and more.

Other popular events include the Heritage Sandy Springs Farmers Market held April through November, and Concerts by the Springs, a free outdoor concert series held in the summer.

CHAPTER 8

EDUCATION

Emory University students studying in Woodruff Library.
Credit: Emory University Photo Video/Bryan Meltz

Overall, the student body in metro Atlanta exceeds 275,000, with the metro area region attracting some of the best and brightest minds in the country. A 2014 study by NerdWallet named Atlanta one of the top 10 cities for college graduates. The talent pool here is deep, which in turn, is helping to drive more companies to establish an Atlanta presence.

New residents will find Atlanta's education market very diverse—offering public, private, and charter school options to meet families' individual needs. Fordham Institute recently ranked Atlanta one of the top 10 cities nationally for "school choice"—a category that includes charter schools, private school vouchers, and public magnet schools. With all this variety, where does a new arrival to metro Atlanta begin?

Leslie Anderson, a mother of four children who came to Atlanta in 2007, advises new residents to begin by asking their real estate agent, who often has basic information about schools, and to read everything they can about the school market. She noted, *"Real estate agents can send you to solid sites that have school rankings and provide what a school's strengths and weaknesses are."* Another important source is current residents or people who have lived in Atlanta.

Anderson, a former education reporter and social worker / advocate for troubled youth, admitted that it was hard to figure out the "pattern" of schools in Atlanta at first since a given public school district can have a lot of variance in terms of performance. Also, because of the shift and growth in Atlanta's population in the last several years, *"redistricting takes place here a lot more frequently than what I've seen in other places."*

If a child has special needs, parents have many options for private schools, noted another mother, Kirstie Price, who came to Atlanta from the Northeast and whose son struggled with dyslexia. She attended local dyslexia parent-support meetings and learned about options. The Metro Atlanta area has several private schools that specialize in educating children with dyslexia or learning differences.

"The public school system is really complicated if your child needs help," she said. Parents need to first define what their child's learning challenge is and get a diagnosis. She used Georgia State University's Psychology Clinic at: www2.gsu.edu/~wwwpsy/clinic/8739.html, which she said enables parents to get their child evaluated for half the price of a private psychologist.

Parents need to start early applying for admission, advised Price. *"If your child is not in the private school system by middle school, he or she may not get into the private school that you want,"* she said.

The average cost of a private school education in Atlanta is $20,000 a year. Price recommends buying tuition insurance, which is 10% of tuition, to cover the investment if the school isn't a fit or if a child must leave due to illness or other issues. Price added that only a handful of schools provide transportation so parents need to plan on driving their child to school.

If a family wants their child to have a diverse education with children from all over the world, they can choose from two international schools. Atlanta also has its share of "big" private schools that give children a more traditional education experience, similar to what they would have in a public school.

"Atlanta has a really good mom population—networking is key," Price said.

Atlanta Parent Magazine publishes its annual Education Guide ([www.issuu.com/atlantaparent/docs/bbos 15 issuu](www.issuu.com/atlantaparent/docs/bbos_15_issuu)) in November/ December. This source for parents seeking a private education for their kids breaks down private schools by who they serve, what they cost, and what area of town they serve, etc. Some valuable information on the various public school systems is also included. The Guide also includes a list of all screenings and immunizations students need, where to receive these services, and how to document everything.

Next are some high-level rankings of the best schools, kindergarten through college, in the metro area, based on data from Great Schools. org. Although the Atlanta Metropolitan Statistical Area is 29 counties large, this book concentrates on communities in the City of Atlanta and Fulton, DeKalb, Gwinnett and Cobb counties.

Rank	Elementary Schools	City
1	Brandon Elementary School	Atlanta
2	Morningside Elementary School	Atlanta
3	Jackson Elementary School	Atlanta
4	Still Elementary School	Powder Springs
5	East Side Elementary School	Marietta
6	Sope Creek Elementary School	Marietta
7	Murdock Elementary School	Marietta
8	Garrison Mill Elementary School	Marietta
9	Baker Elementary School	Acworth
10	Ford Elementary School	Acworth
Rank	Middle Schools	City
1	Dodgen Middle School	Marietta
2	Dickerson Middle School	Marietta
3	River Trail Middle School	Duluth
4	Webb Bridge Middle School	Alpharetta
5	Northwestern Middle School	Alpharetta
6	Crabapple Middle School	Roswell
7	Alton C. Crews Middle School	Lawrenceville
8	Autrey Mill Middle School	Alpharetta
9	Amana Academy	Alpharetta
10	Glenn C. Jones Middle School	Buford
Rank	High Schools	City
1	Buford High School	Buford
2	Lassiter High School	Marietta
3	Harrison High School	Kennesaw
4	Milton High School	Alpharetta
5	Chattahoochee High School	Alpharetta
6	North Gwinnett High School	Suwanee
7	Brookwood High School	Snellville
8	Northview High School	Johns Creek
9	DeKalb Early College Academy	Stone Mountain
10	Fulton Science Academy High School	Alpharetta

Source: www.greatschool.com/georgia/atlanta/schools/

How Atlanta High Schools Rank Nationally

U.S. News & World Report's annual list of the top-performing high schools in the country ranked Gwinnett School of Mathematics,

Science, and Technology as the Peach State's best. Georgia is No. 12 in the nation for best high schools with 19 gold medal schools and 45 silver medal schools. Of the top 10 schools in Georgia, seven are in the metro Atlanta area. Of those seven, four are in North Fulton, one was in East Cobb, one was in Gwinnett, and one was in DeKalb. To be eligible for a state ranking, the school had to earn a national gold or silver medal for excellence. Rankings are based on student-teacher ratio, college readiness, and mathematics, and English proficiency.

Georgia's Title I schools—those exhibiting the greatest need for additional support—are among the lowest 5% in the state in terms of performance. Fifteen of these schools are in City of Atlanta Public Schools, ten are in south DeKalb, three are located in south Fulton, three are in Clayton, two are in Gwinnett, and one is in south Cobb.

Colleges and Universities

Founded in 1835, Oglethorpe University is among the top liberal arts universities in the country. Credit: Jeff Roffman

The University System of Georgia provides excellent educational opportunities at its 30 institutions for those seeking a bachelors, masters or doctorate degrees.

The Technical College System of Georgia has 22 colleges and locations throughout the state that are accessible, affordable, and accredited.

Ninety-eight percent of TCSG graduates find employment or continue in higher education.

Metro Atlanta schools have made a number of educational rankings by *U.S. News and World Report*. Of the nation's top 199 national universities for 2016, Emory University tied for #21, Georgia Tech was #36, and UGA tied for #61. Clark Atlanta University and Georgia State University made this list, but their ratings were not published.

Agnes Scott College tied for #67 amongst national liberal arts colleges in the same report. Spelman College was tied for #72, Morehouse College tied for #148, and Oglethorpe University tied for #167.

Young people interested in engineering studies have some excellent options in metro Atlanta. According to *U.S. News and World Report*, Georgia Institute of Technology (Georgia Tech) tied for #6 amongst undergraduate engineering programs with doctoral degrees, while Spelman College was #1 amongst historically black colleges and universities followed by Morehouse College (#4) and Clark Atlanta (#19).

In 2014, Georgia Tech was ranked #1 smartest public college by *Business Insider* magazine and has the largest aerospace engineering program in the nation.

Graduate Schools

The best graduate schools in metro Atlanta, according to *U.S. New and World Report*, were Emory University (tied for #21 amongst graduate business schools), Georgia Tech (tied for #30), and UGA (tied for #53). Four additional schools—Clark Atlanta, UGA, Kennesaw State, and Mercer Atlanta—made the list but were not rated for undisclosed reasons.

Georgia's Hope Scholarship

Unfortunately, the cost of attending a Georgia college or university is increasing. In fact, Georgia ranks No. 2 in highest average tuition increase during the last five years, jumping by 48% since 2010, according to a new Bloomberg report citing data from the Urban Institute.

Fortunately, Georgia offers the HOPE (Helping Outstanding Pupils Educationally) Scholarship for Georgia high schools students who have a 3.0 GPA or better and want to attend a HOPE-eligible school or a school within the University System of Georgia. The 20-year-old scholarship is funded entirely by the Georgia Lottery for Education.

The National Association of State Student Grant and Aid Programs finds that Georgia awards more scholarship dollars to its college students than any other state except South Carolina. HOPE has ensured that more Georgians graduate from college—over the past two decades, Georgia college grads increased from 19 to 28 percent. And they tend to stay here, too. *Atlanta Magazine* reported in 2014 that a decade after HOPE's debut, more than 40 percent of Georgia high school seniors who scored between 1400 and 1490 on the SAT elected to stay in-state for college—double the rate before the scholarship existed.

Unfortunately, due to rising college costs, HOPE used to cover a large portion of expenses, but now only covers a small portion at many schools. The rigor required for the HOPE beyond the GPA requirements is also increasing. Students must maintain a 3.0 GPA in college to maintain the HOPE.

For students demonstrating even higher academic performance (3.7 GPA or better, minimum SAT score, etc.), Georgia offers the ZELL, or Zell Miller Scholarship. These scholarships cover a larger portion of expenses than HOPE does. Students must maintain a 3.3 GPA or better in college to maintain the ZELL.

Veterans

Nearly 18,000 Georgia veterans are taking advantage of their GI education benefits. They also are eligible for HOPE, Zell Miller, and Georgia's Strategic Industries Workforce Development Grant Awards. Veterans receive in-state tuition for up to three years after leaving the military. Admissions fees are also waived for military using tuition assistance.

All state schools offer online distance learning opportunities and many offer on-campus veteran centers. For veterans going into the workforce, the Georgia Department of Labor offers priority employment services provided by veterans' specialists throughout a statewide network of career centers. There's one near every military base in Georgia. The free service includes job search and resume assistance, as well as finding veteran-friendly employers.

Adult & Community Education

Many adults look to continuing education programs to improve their career opportunities or to prepare for further education. In the Atlanta area, flexible programs are available to adult learners at several of the city's colleges and universities. In addition, many Park & Recreation Departments offer community classes, as well.

Kennesaw State University's College of Continuing Education and Professional Services has one of Georgia's largest programs, with 17,000 annual enrollments. According to the College's dean, Barbara Calhoun, many working people in metro Atlanta are opting for certificate programs to stay competitive in a fast-changing job environment in lieu of pursuing a four-year or advanced degree.

"Continuous lifelong learning is more critical now than ever before," she said, pointing to the growth in the film, music, and technology industries in Atlanta, as well as healthcare and transportation and logistics. *"The most in-demand jobs in Atlanta are software developers and engineers followed by truck drivers and certified nursing assistants."*

Continuous learning is also important to the many retirees and seniors living in the metro area. Atlanta's popularity as a retirement spot is evident by the number of new constructions for 50 and older communities and by rankings such as NerdWallet naming Atlanta-Sandy Springs-Marietta metro area #6 in America's fastest-growing retirement places in 2014.

Calhoun said that Kennesaw's program has over 3,000 people enrolled in its Osher Lifelong Learning Institute (OLLI), which offers courses to adults age 50 and older in designated classroom spaces and a computer lab. Many older Atlantans are interested in courses that teach them how to use technology, she explained.

Here's a snapshot of three of the largest continuing education programs in metro Atlanta:

Georgia Tech's Continuing & Professional Education Programs

Georgia Tech is a public school that offers continuing education classes through its division of Professional Education. The school has 28 certificate programs for adults and more than 1,000 available courses. Certificate programs are available in several subjects, including defense technology, project management, power systems, and supply chain and logistics.

- Website: www.pe.gatech.edu

Emory University's Continuing Education Programs

Emory University is a private institution that provides continuing education opportunities through its Center for Lifelong Learning. The school offers 20 certificate programs and dozens of professional development and personal enrichment classes. Emory offers flexible scheduling, which can allow working professionals to take advantage of course offerings.

- Website: www.ece.emory.edu/courses_and_certificates/index.html

Kennesaw State University's Continuing Education Programs

Kennesaw State University is Georgia's third-largest university and is located north of Atlanta. It offers more than 50 professional certificate programs through its College of Continuing and Professional Education, reaching 17,000 students a year.

- Website: www.ccpe.kennesaw.edu

Helpful Links:

The Atlanta School Guide – www.atlantaschoolguide.com – published by Killam Publishing, this digital and print publication provides detailed, year-round information to help direct parents to the schools and educational resources that best fit their family's needs..

***Atlanta Magazine* Independent School Guide 2015/16** – www. atlantamagazine.com/school-guide-2015 – The 2015 School Guide gives parents detailed information about tuition, arts programs, athletics, AP classes, and more for 75 metro-area independent schools. Clicking on a school name in the online digital directory lets parents see the grades served, total number of students, average class size, annual tuition costs, teacher retention rates and other information.

GA College 411 – www.secure.gacollege411.org/Homedefault.aspx – This website, managed by the Georgia Student Finance Commission, provides financial aid and college and career planning services for students from middle school through college, as well as guidance for adults and military members.

***Atlanta Journal Constitution's* Get Schooled** Blog and Georgia School News – www.getschooled.blog.ajc.com and www.ajc.com/news/GaSchoolNews

CHAPTER 9

CONNECTING WITH THE COMMUNITY

Attendees at TAG's STEM Education Awards.
Credit: ByteGraph Productions

Many Atlantans are natural connectors active in their communities. And new residents don't have to look far to get involved in organizations to meet people with similar interests, strengthen their personal and professional networks, and support worthwhile organizations.

"Greater Atlanta offers an abundance of wonderful organizations and associations for men and women who want to connect both socially and professionally. Newcomers will find southern hospitality throughout a wide variety of networking opportunities," noted Bonnie Ross-Parker, CEO/Founder of Xperience Connections, which holds networking

events for women business owners in 16 locations throughout metro Atlanta.

For the last four years, the Georgia Center for Nonprofits has hosted what it calls "the annual flash mob of giving" – Georgia Gives Day. From midnight to midnight every November 12, donors statewide visit GAgivesday.org and give to their favorites of more than 2,000 participating nonprofits.

The event *"highlights the important work of local nonprofits in sustaining and building our communities while also helping Georgians discover and connect with organizations that share their passions,"* said Karen Beavor, president and CEO of the Georgia Center for Nonprofits.

Associations & Community Organizations

To find organizations meeting in your area, visit Community Organization MeetUps in Atlanta at: www.communityorg.meetup. com/cities/us/ga/atlanta

Below is a snapshot of some of a few leading associations and community organizations:

Hands On Atlanta – www.handsonatlanta.org – This volunteer-driven organization helps individuals, families, corporate, and community groups strengthen Greater Atlanta through service at more than 400 nonprofit organizations and schools. Volunteers work every day of the year tutoring and mentoring children, helping individuals and families make pathways out of poverty, improving Atlanta's environment, and more. Hands On Atlanta is an affiliate of the Hands On Network, an association of 250 volunteer service organizations across 16 countries.

The Kiwanis Club of Atlanta – www.kiwanisatlanta.org – Members have been active in the Atlanta community since 1915 embracing the motto, "Learn, Serve, Connect." Weekly luncheon meetings feature diverse speakers and members also give back to the community through various charitable organizations.

Technology Association of Georgia – www.tagonline.org/about – TAG's mission is to educate, promote, influence, and unite Georgia's technology community to foster an innovative and connected marketplace that stimulates and enhances Georgia's tech-based economy. This 30,000-plus member organization holds more than 200 events a year and has 34 societies. It also advocates for positive public policy change, working with government leaders to develop and enact the policies and legislation that will bolster the growth of Georgia's technology community.

Faith-based Organizations

Atlanta's historic Ebenezer Baptist Church

The Atlanta metro area has abundant worship and fellowship options to choose from.

For Christians, Baptist churches are by far the most numerous, ranging from neighborhood churches with memberships under 100 to megachurches with memberships over ten thousand. Perhaps the most historic church in Atlanta is Ebenezer Baptist. The "Heritage Sanctuary" where Dr. Martin Luther King Jr. was pastor is part of the National Park Service's historic site. Methodist, Presbyterian, Lutheran, and Episcopal churches are in each community, as well as many other Christian and non-denominational options.

For Catholics, the Archdiocese of Atlanta has numerous Parishes around metro Atlanta and north Georgia.

For Jewish residents, several dozen temples and synagogues dot the metro Atlanta area. In addition, the Marcus Jewish Community Center in Dunwoody is one of the nation's largest JCC in the country, founded in part by Home Depot founders Bernie Marcus and Arthur Blank.

Many areas of metro Atlanta are also served by mosques and gurdwaras (Sikh temples). Essentially, those of every religious faith can find a worship and fellowship home in metro Atlanta and likely have several choices nearby.

Media

Atlanta Press Club photo of the Governor Debates
Credit: Sonia Lemos

Atlanta has always served as a vibrant media center, home to national news brands such as CNN, Turner Broadcasting, The Weather Channel, and a host of local radio, TV, and magazine media outlets. In fact, metro Atlanta is the ninth-largest media market in the United States, according to Nielson Media Research.

"We have four strong network affiliate television stations: a daily newspaper that's been here for 150 years, The Atlanta Journal-Constitution; and a number of radio stations, including two stations that offer National

Public Radio (NPR) content," said veteran Atlanta public relations expert Mitch Leff. *"Atlanta probably has more journalists here than most cities in the country other than New York, Chicago, LA, and a couple of other cities."*

Leff, who created Leff's Atlanta Media, a database of all Atlanta-based press, explained that the city has a strong Associated Press bureau, as well as bureaus for *The Washington Post,* the *Wall Street Journal* and Bloomberg News. The three major broadcast networks, CNN, and Fox News are all present, too. CNN's Atlanta headquarters is the largest of CNN's 48 bureaus worldwide.

News outlets serving African-American, Hispanic, and Asian audiences are plentiful, including *The Atlanta Daily World,* Atlanta's oldest continuously published black newspaper, and Hispanic-focused *Mundo Hispanico.* The top source for business news is the *Atlanta Business Chronicle,* published weekly by American City Business Journals. Its annual Book of Lists comes out every December.

The *Atlanta Journal-Constitution* and the *Gwinnett Daily Post* have the highest readership in the state, according to media database provider, Cision, and its top 10 newspapers in Georgia based on circulation. The *Marietta Daily Journal* rounded out the list at number ten. Residents turn to the non-daily newspaper, *Creative Loafing,* the Southeast's largest alt-weekly, for entertainment and the latest happenings. Readers cast votes every year to honor their favorite people, places, foods, and more in *Creative Loafing's* annual Best of Atlanta issue, out in September.

"We have innovative and strong writing going on outside the mainstream media—I think that's what makes Atlanta's media market really interesting," Leff noted, pointing to online-only publications such as *The Bitter Southerner,* Artsatl.com, and *Decaturish.* For political and business commentary, there is *The Saporta Report,* the weekly online news site of Maria Saporta, a former *Atlanta Journal-Constitution* columnist who contributes to the *Atlanta Business Chronicle* as well.

Atlanta maintains a robust market for magazine publishers of all sizes and interests, from travel to lifestyle, entertainment and fashion. *Atlanta* magazine, started in 1961, remains the dominant monthly in terms of readership; its "Best of Atlanta" annual guide features the best restaurants, shops, services and entertainment the city has to offer. *Georgia Trend* has covered Georgia business, politics and economic development since 1985. Social magazines range from *Atlanta Social Season* to *The Atlantan* and *Jezebel Magazine,* while intown and other geographically targeted magazines include *Vinings Lifestyle, Cobb In Focus, Simply Buckhead, Points North Atlanta* and *Gwinnett Magazine.*

In terms of the radio market, the most prominent station is Atlanta WSB-AM 750, which was ranked #9 in Nielson Audio's top 10 radio stations in the U.S., with 1.2 million listeners.

"WSB is the ratings powerhouse here in Atlanta," said Leff. *"But there are several other players for local radio news, offering both short and long-form programming."*

Other notable stations include News Radio 106.7 | WYAY-FM, a news talk radio station, and WABE, one of two NPR stations in Atlanta. Leff said that WABE in the past year has added more staff and programming. The second NPR station, Georgia Public Broadcasting, recently entered into an agreement to take over a part of Georgia State's radio station, which has enhanced Georgia Public Radio's Atlanta presence.

For a list of most of Atlanta's radio stations, Rodney Ho, *Atlanta Journal-Constitution* blogger and columnist, maintains a list on his *Radio & TV Talk* blog at: www.radiotvtalk.blog.ajc.com/atlanta-radio-station-links.

Leff's advice for news consumers as they move into metro Atlanta is straightforward: *"Be a diverse reader. Don't get your news from just one source; listen to radio stations, watch different TV stations; read different news sources."*

Television Stations at a Glance

The following are the main Atlanta-area TV stations, as compiled by StationIndex.com:

Name	Affiliate of...	Website
WSB	ABC	www.wsbtv.com
WGCL	CBS	www.cbsatlanta.com
WAGA	Fox	www.myfoxatlanta.com
WXIA	NBC	www.11alive.com
WUPA	CW	cwatlanta.cbslocal.com
WGTV	GA Public Broadcasting	www.gpb.org
WPBA	GA Public Broadcasting	www.wpba.org
WPCH	independent	www.peachtreetv.com
WATL	Independent	www.myatltv.com
WHSG	TBN	www.tbn.org
WATC	Independent - Religious	www.watc.tv

Source: www.stationindex.com/tv/markets/atlanta

Voting

In Georgia, general voter registration deadlines are thirty days prior to an election. Georgia also has "open registration"—meaning residents self-select at the polls, choosing either a Democrat or Republican ballot. All voters should allow forty-five days for absentee voting by mail and should request an absentee ballot at their county elections office. The state also offers in-person voting in advance of an election. This option occurs three weeks prior to an election in the county a voter resides in.

Anyone with a Georgia driver's license can register to vote online at www.sos.ga.gov. To verify registration, click Check Voter Registration Status on that same page. The easiest way to register to vote is to do it at the same time residents get their Georgia driver's license.

The League of Women Voters of Georgia publishes several Voter's Guides in conjunction with *The Atlanta-Journal Constitution* thirty days before most key elections. Guides for the Georgia Primary in May are typically available in mid-April. The general election Guide is available in early October, a month before Atlantans head to the polls. The Voter's Guide features each candidate running for office and verbatim responses to personal and issues questions. For more information and free resources, including the Guide to Voting in Georgia, visit the League of Women Voters of Georgia website at: www.lwvga.org.

CHAPTER 10

ENDLESS THINGS TO DO

**The majestic Beluga whales in Georgia Aquarium's
Georgia-Pacific Cold Water Quest.
Credit: Georgia Aquarium**

The ATL, the city's new hip nickname, offers an amazing mix of entertainment options for Atlanta's diverse demographic. Debbie Michaud, editor-in-chief of *Creative Loafing Atlanta*, the city's alternative weekly, noted that Atlanta's entertainment scene means a lot of different things to different groups.

It's a big convention town with a downtown offering a lot of large tourist attractions—everything from the World of Coca-Cola, to Centennial Olympic Park, to Phillips Arena, to the Georgia Aquarium and SkyView Atlanta, the city's 200-foot tall Ferris wheel.

121

Zoo Atlanta, located in historic Grant Park, is one of only four zoos in the United States housing giant pandas and the only zoo in the country to have twin giant panda cubs.

For sports fans, Atlanta hosts six professional sports teams. Two teams will have new digs soon: the Atlanta Falcons NFL team will move into the new $1.2 billion Mercedes-Benz Stadium downtown by 2017, while the city's Major League Baseball team, the Atlanta Braves, will call the new $1.1 billion SunTrust Park in Cobb County home in the 2017 season. Atlanta's new Major League Soccer (MLS) team, the Atlanta United FC, will debut in 2017 at the Mercedes-Benz Stadium. Basketball season brings fans to Phillips Arena for the city's NBA and WNBA teams, the Atlanta Hawks and Atlanta Dream.

Atlanta is also a "con mecca," hosting five sci-fi and fantasy conventions each year, including Dragon*Con, which drew 85,000 people over Labor Day weekend 2015. The volume of cons, along with the number of video game stores (one per every 16,000 residents) earned Atlanta the moniker, the nerdiest city in America, according to real estate blogger Movoto.

Chef-driven Dining and Farmer's Markets

Another important pastime for Atlantans is dining options. According to Michaud, *"the restaurant scene in Atlanta has exploded in terms of the chef-driven trend that is prevalent all over the country. Atlanta used to be more chain- and high-end fine-dining focused, but now neighborhoods have highly individualized and unique restaurants run by chefs who want to buy ingredients as locally as possible or even grow their own food."*

"An offshoot of that is there is a huge farmer's market culture in Atlanta," added Michaud, explaining that the city has developed a robust farmer's market community over the last two decades. Morningside Farmers Market was Atlanta's first 100-percent organic community farmers market when it started in 1995. It was followed by Decatur Farmers Market in 2000, Piedmont Park Green Market in 2003, and East Atlanta Village Farmers Market in 2006, to name a few.

There also are a ton of craft cocktail bars in the city—with even restaurants becoming very craft-cocktail oriented. *"Over the last decade, craft cocktails have become increasingly popular, in Atlanta and across the country, with bartenders becoming interested in the alchemy of drink-making and building a modern cocktail movement,"* said Michaud.

Shopping for fresh herbs and produce at East Atlanta Village Farmers Market. Credit: Jenna Shea Photography

Where to Go to Find Great Restaurants

Atlanta Magazine publishes its annual list of the 50 Best Restaurants in Atlanta every January. See current and previous lists here: www.atlantamagazine.com/50bestrestaurants.

The magazine also regularly covers restaurants in its Food & Drink column: www.atlantamagazine.com/food-drink.

Creative Loafing's Atlanta City Guide includes both regular features on the dining scene in Atlanta and a handy pull-down search menu under its Dining tab, with categories such as "bakery," "barbecue," "Indian" or "New American." See: www.clatl.com/atlanta/NeighborhoodGuide.

Zagat's Atlanta online rates restaurants by food, décor, service and cost, and also publishes features and lists. Recent articles of note:

Atlanta's Best Restaurants (Bones Steakhouse in Buckhead topped the list) www.zagat.com/l/atlanta/best-food-in-atlanta.

Atlanta's Most Popular Restaurants (The Varsity, Atlanta Fish Market, Ray's on the River, and Fellini's were top finishers) www.zagat.com/l/atlanta/most-popular-in-atlanta.

Where to Go to Find Great Bars

The same online and print publications listed above for restaurants also provide feature articles, reviews, and rankings for drinking establishments throughout Atlanta (for example, a recent feature from Zagat highlighted "The 10 Hottest New Bars in Atlanta": www.zagat.com/b/atlanta/the-10-hottest-new-bars-in-atlanta).

New arrivals to the city wishing to quench their thirst may first wish to peruse *Thirsty South*, a drink blog founded in 2011 by Brad Kaplan, a *Creative Loafing* contributing food writer. Dedicated "to all things drinking well, in Atlanta and beyond," the site's *Thirsty Guide to Atlanta* (www.thirstysouth.com/thirsty-guide-to-atlanta), includes a breakdown of Atlanta area:

Cocktails & Whiskey Bars

Liquor Stores

Beer Bars

Beer Shops

Wine Selections, Restaurants & Bars

Wine Shops

Coffee Bars & Roasters

The Music Scene

Atlanta's music scene is equally varied, from the highly regarded Atlanta Symphony and the Atlanta Pops to its vibrant country scene, and status as the hip-hop capital of the U.S. There also is a thriving metal and indie-rock (or garage rock) scene.

"Atlanta's got real diversity in its music offerings—hip hop, R&B, soul, garage rock, indie rock, metal, punk, and you have a number of independent venues around town," noted Michaud.

Music fans have the choice of going to large settings like Philips Arena, Woodruff Arts Center, and the outdoor Chastain Amphitheater to more intimate locales such as the Tabernacle and Variety Playhouse.

"The other aspect of the music scene in Atlanta is just the rise of the music festival over the last few years," said Michaud. *"We have Music Midtown. We have Shaky Knees, which does indie rock, and they have two offshoots, Shaky Boots, which was started up in Kennesaw in the last year or two focused on country, and Shaky Beats, which blends electronic and hip-hop."*

For a list of Atlanta music venues, go to:

www.atlantamusicguide.com/more-content/atlanta-venues

City of Festivals

**Opening Night for the 2015 Atlanta Jewish Film Festival
at the Cobb Energy Performing Arts Centre.
Credit: Duane Storky**

As already noted in the neighborhood spotlights, Atlanta is a major festival town, with the mild climate and plentiful trees enabling communities to host festivals and events year-round. *"What distinguishes Atlanta from other places is its neighborhoods—there's a fierce pride people have intown and outside the Perimeter,"* Michaud said.

One of the city's most popular events is the Atlanta Dogwood Festival, an arts and crafts gathering held in Piedmont Park each spring, when the native dogwoods are in bloom.

Atlanta Streets Alive, inspired by the ciclovía in Bogotá, Colombia, closes city streets to car traffic to allow people to participate in health and community-oriented activities, such as bicycling, strolling, skating, people-watching, tango, yoga, hula hooping, and break dancing.

Atlanta is home to one of the nation's largest gay pride festivals, Atlanta Pride, as well as what is billed as the world's largest black gay pride celebration, Atlanta Black Pride.

Given Georgia's growing prominence in filmmaking, it's no surprise the city has been a major center for film festivals for well over a decade. A few notable ones for new residents who love film include:

- Atlanta Film Festival, an Academy Award qualifying, international film festival held every April that showcases a diverse range of independent films, including genre films such as horror and sci-fi

- The Atlanta Jewish Film Festival, the largest Jewish film festival in the world , held over twenty-three days in January and February

- The Atlanta Movie Festival, in its 40th year in 2016 and including not just a festival but year-round advance screenings of indie films for members

- The Atlanta Asian Film Festival, the largest Asian film festival in the South, in its 12th year in 2016

- Atlanta's Out on Film, one of the oldest LGBT film festivals in the country

- The Atlanta Underground Film Festival, a forum where independent filmmakers thrive outside the mainstream celebrating its 13th year in 2016

- The Atlanta International Documentary Film Festival, an annual celebration of the best in independent documentary film and video, in its 11th year in 2016

- Buried Alive Film Fest, Atlanta's premier horror film festival

Film Tourism

The impact of Hollywood on Atlanta's entertainment scene is evident by the rise of film tourism (reported in the Hollywood of the South chapter), as well as the announcement of Avatron Park, the first venue to host "Hunger Games"-themed attractions. It is scheduled to open off Red Top Mountain Road, an hour north of Atlanta, in January 2019.

Major Historical Sites and Cultural Centers

In addition to The Carter Center and The Martin Luther King, Jr. Center for Nonviolent Social Change ("The King Center") in downtown Atlanta, there are numerous art galleries and museums, many of which are concentrated in Midtown and Buckhead:

- High Museum of Art (Midtown)
  www.high.org
- Museum of Design Atlanta (Midtown)

  www.museumofdesign.org
- Museum of Contemporary Art of Georgia (Buckhead) –
  www.mocaga.org
- Atlanta Contemporary (Midtown)

  www.atlantacontemporary.org
- Atlanta History Center (Buckhead)

  www.atlantahistorycenter.com
- Fernbank Museum of Natural History (Druid Hills)
  www.fernbankmuseum.org
- World of Coca-Cola (Atlanta)
  www.worldofcoca-cola.com

Growing DIY Arts Culture

Michaud said she is particularly excited about the strong DIY culture evident in Atlanta. *"South downtown is on the verge of a great resurgence,"* Michaud said. For example, Mammal Gallery on South Broad Street is a DIY artists' space that hosts music and art events. Eyedrum, an artists' collective currently renovating a long-vacant 1920's space in south downtown, *"is the granddaddy of underground experimental art in Atlanta,"* she added.

Atlanta has long had a vibrant graffiti culture, but now it's being recognized for its public art through successful programs such as Elevate, its annual, week-long public art festival as well as the city's Living Walls and Art on the Beltline programs.

Sports & Fitness

An ALTA mixed doubles match in Marietta.
Credit: Suzanne Dent, ALTA

One of the best sources to learn about Atlanta's many sports leagues is visiting the Atlanta Sports and Social Club website, www. atlantasportandsocialclub.com. The club organizes a variety of adult recreational sports leagues in the Atlanta area, including basketball, bowling, flag football, soccer, softball, kickball, ultimate Frisbee, and volleyball. The club also organizes social events throughout the year. These include activities like Atlanta Field Day, the National Beer Mile series, and several sports tournaments.

Below are a few of Atlanta's established adult sports institutions and what makes them unique:

- **Atlanta Lawn and Tennis Association** – ALTA has about 70,000 members annually, including adults and juniors. These members pay modest annual dues and can play in multiple leagues during the year. ALTA is considered the largest tennis organization in the country.

- **Atlanta Track Club** – This member-based nonprofit centered around running is committed to creating an active and healthy Atlanta through world-class events, training programs, and community outreach activities. With more than 24,000 members, Atlanta Track Club is the second-largest running organization in the United States. Today, the club puts on over 30 events a year throughout the Atlanta area, including the AJC Peachtree Road Race, the largest 10K in the world and a Fourth of July tradition. Some 60,000 participants as young as 10 and as old as 95 participated in 2015, drawing approximately 200,000 spectators.

- **Atlanta Rowing Club** – This master's level rowing club with 215 members is based in Roswell on the Chattahoochee River. It started in 1974 on Stone Mountain Lake before moving to Roswell in the 1980s. About 60% of the members are women and members range in age between 20 and 75. The Club offers a Learn to Row program and has a fleet of 35 boats. Roswell also hosts two high school rowing programs— the Atlanta Junior Rowing Association and the St. Andrews Rowing Club—and two college teams, Georgia Tech and Georgia State University.

Fresh Air

New residents to Atlanta have a multitude of outdoor options to stay active and take in Atlanta's diverse landscapes. Because of the city's mild climate, many of these outdoorsy activities are enjoyed year-round.

"We're out on the trail in every season. I especially love the long length of Georgia's most beautiful seasons, the spring and fall," said Eric Champlin, editor and founder of Atlanta Trails, an online magazine

with more than 1.5 million readers that helps people find outdoor adventures in Atlanta and throughout Georgia.

While Atlanta's summers are hot and humid, the city's proximity to mountains enables people to escape the heat and be up at a higher elevation within a few hours.

An Ohio native who moved to Atlanta in 1999, Champlin recalled how stunned he was by the state's landscape diversity featuring everything from coastal plains to southern Appalachian Mountains, from waterfalls to river valleys. There also are numerous places to backpack on trails and off trails.

**Eric Champlin with his dog, Jake, on the Appalachian Trail.
Credit: Atlanta Trails**

"Within a short drive you can find yourself in so many diverse areas," he said. Driving less than a half-hour to the west, residents can explore Sweetwater Creek, a beautiful river valley filled with whitewater and small waterfalls. Driving a half hour to the east, they can explore Arabia Mountain and Stone Mountain. Two hours south of Atlanta is Providence Canyon, a place known as Georgia's "Little Grand Canyon."

Stone Mountain Park offers one of the best panoramic views of Atlanta, and features the world's largest exposed mass of granite. The 90-by-190-foot Civil War sculpture sandblasted from the face of the mountain rises four hundred feet above the ground.

"I love living in Atlanta, with all that a big city offers, but yet being able to set my compass in any direction and find amazing (and diverse!) hiking, camping, biking or paddling adventures," said Champlin, who takes his rescue dog, Jake, on every outdoor excursion.

Atlanta Trails has covered more than 200 of Georgia's best trails, said Champlin, who also confessed that *"there are so many more to cover, thanks to Georgia's amazing trail systems."* One of the site's more popular articles is its list of top ten favorite Atlanta hiking trails: www.atlantatrails.com/hiking-trails/atlantas-best-hiking-trails-our-top-10-favorite-hikes.

Below, Champlin shares five places every new Atlantan should experience.

Atlanta Trails' Top 5 Metro Atlanta Outdoor Adventures for New Residents:

The Chattahoochee River offers Atlantans plenty of recreational options.

#1 Chattahoochee River National Recreation Area – *"A lot of Atlanta natives don't realize we have several extensions of the National Park Service near Atlanta. The Chattahoochee River National Recreation Area spans from Lake Lanier down to the I-285/Perimeter. There are so many hiking and running trails on the Chattahoochee. It also was the first designated National Water Trail in the country, and it's a great place to kayak, canoe, raft or tube in the summer."*

#2 Sweetwater Creek State Park – *"It's Georgia's closest state park near Atlanta, and it really gives you the feeling of being hours outside of the city in a beautiful, rugged landscape. The park added a yurt village in 2015, a collection of large wood-frame and canvas tents. Sleeping in a yurt is like camping, but without the hassle of packing a tent, and the yurts have electricity, hardwood floors, a dining table and beds with comfortable mattresses. It's a really cool camping experience for families."*

#3 Arabia Mountain National Heritage Area – *"This hidden gem was once a granite quarry, and now offers more than thirty miles of paved biking trails and many miles of fantastic hiking trails. The trails wind through former quarry areas, through wide expanses of granite, around beautiful small lakes, through pine forests and to a mountain summit. The most popular trail climbs up Arabia Mountain, a large rounded granite dome. At the top of the mountain, you'll find shallow pools and craters that collect water after a rain, home to a wide diversity of rare and unusual plants. The mountaintop is so unique it's easy to forget you're a half hour from Atlanta."*

#4 The Atlanta Beltline – *"It's absolutely wonderful for a run, stroll or a bike ride. The Beltline has its own culture—it's not only a place to get out and exercise, but also a great place to run into friends, chat, and grab a bite at a restaurant along the trail. The newly-opened Ponce City Market on the Eastside Trail even has a bike valet, making it a great stop to shop or dine along the trail."*

#5 Silver Comet Tail – *"It's such an amazing long-distance biking, running and skating trail, close to the city. The Silver Comet Trail runs over sixty miles, from the Smyrna area to the Alabama border, where it continues on as the Chief Ladiga Trail. Thanks to its railway history, it follows a gentle grade, so there are very few hills to climb, making for a really great run or long-distance bike ride. It's also wonderfully scenic. The trail travels through communities and forests, over raised train trestles, and it dips down into old railway tunnels below roads. Parallel to the Silver Comet, there are mountain-biking trails and horse-riding trails, too."*

Event Calendars

There are numerous online calendars new residents can use to find events in Atlanta. A few of the major ones include:

The Atlanta Journal-Constitution's Access Atlanta:
www.accessatlanta.com

Atlanta Convention & Visitors Bureau – Events:
www.atlanta.net/events

Eventful: www.atlanta.eventful.com/events

Creative Loafing Atlanta's Search Events:
www.clatl.com

CHAPTER 11

THE ECONOMY

Credit: The Home Depot

Few cities can boast the number of opportunities for young people starting their careers or for entrepreneurs and seasoned professionals to progress and advance in their work, especially in the aerospace, automotive, call center, entertainment, financial tech, health IT, and logistics and transportation sectors.

In December 2015, for the third consecutive year, Georgia was ranked the best state in the nation for business by *Site Selection* magazine.

In addition, Metro Atlanta is one of only three major metros to add more than a million people between 2000 and 2010, according to Mike Carnathan of the Atlanta Regional Commission.

An affordable cost of living, temperate climate, and proximity to strong colleges and universities has made Atlanta a draw for many Fortune 500 companies to set up operations or headquarters here, including NCR and Mercedes-Benz of North America.

According to Stephen Cannon, former president and CEO of Mercedes-Benz of North America, who played a pivotal role in relocating the automaker to Atlanta, *"Mercedes-Benz is a premier brand which deserves a premier setting. Our ambition is to be more than just a great car company—we want to be among the best companies in the world, and Atlanta will serve as the perfect foundation to foster that ambition for the future. We are proud to call Atlanta home."*

As the table that follows shows, eighteen Fortune 500® headquarters firms now call Atlanta their home base. So many firms are moving their headquarters here that Atlanta Mayor Kasim Reed has dubbed the city the "New Headquarters Capital" in an op-ed published in a special Georgia supplement of *Newsweek Magazine*.

METRO ATLANTA FORTUNE 500 HEADQUARTERS:

ATL Rank	Fortune 500 Rank	Company
1	33	The Home Depot
2	47	United Parcel Service
3	63	The Coca-Cola Company
4	73	Delta Air Lines
5	163	Southern Company
6	199	Genuine Parts Company
7	265	First Data Corporation
8	293	Rock-Tenn Company
9	296	AGCO Corporation
10	316	HD Supply Holdings
11	327	SunTrust Banks
12	368	Coca-Cola Enterprises
13	412	NCR Corporation
14	450	Asbury Automotive Group
15	453	PulteGroup
16	455	Newell Rubbermaid
17	465	AGL Resources
18	492	Arris Group

Source: 2015 FORTUNE 500/1000, *Fortune Magazine*, June 4, 2015

"Atlanta has become one of the on-fire areas for getting a job across the country. It's very desirable now," said Margot King, a thirty-five-

year Atlanta resident and a nationally recognized pioneer in talent acquisition.

King explained that Atlanta has always served as a mecca for Fortune 500 companies to set up a presence in the Southeast. But, it's the booming film and technology sectors that have caught her attention in recent years (See chapter, Hollywood of the South, to learn what's driving the entertainment sector to Atlanta.).

"Atlanta has become a real incubator of new talent, ideas, and technology— that's what has spearheaded its growth," she said, describing Atlanta as another "Silicon Valley."

According to data from the Technology Association of Georgia (TAG), there have been 25,000 new technology jobs added to the Peach State from 2010 to 2014. As previously noted, software engineers and programmers are the most in-demand positions, said Barbara Calhoun, dean of Kennesaw State University's College of Continuing Education and Professional Services.

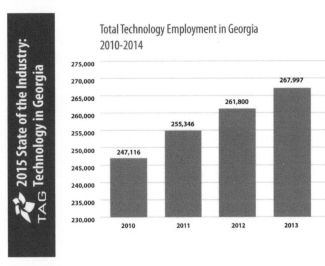

Tino Mantella, president and CEO of TAG, explained that one of the keys to the metro area and the state's acceleration is the growth of technology clusters. *"There have been a lot of studies that show that when you get critical mass, you can hold your talent here and bring in new talent. There's more investment,"* he said.

According to the 2014 Technology Decision Makers Survey, 70 percent of respondents said there are advantages to operating within a Georgia technology cluster, including: access to talent; access to support resources; and collaboration and networking opportunities. The survey also found more focus is needed to link up to the state's universities, incubators, and funding sources to enhance access to resources and support.

Mantella cited two key clusters—financial tech and health IT (HIT), both of which depend largely on processing transactions. Mantella said that 75% of all financial payments flow through Atlanta, and that top employers include: Equifax, First Data, Fiserv, NCR, and TSYS.

Often called the nation's health IT capital, Atlanta is home to more than 225 HIT companies, which employ more than 30,000 Georgians. Some of the largest HIT employers are McKesson Technology Solutions, MedAssets, HealthPort, Greenway Health, and Navicure, which all benefit from the metro area's robust telecommunications infrastructure and academic institutions. The HIT presence has helped elevate Atlanta to the forefront of consumer digital health.

"The nice thing about Georgia and Atlanta is there's a good balance here," said Mantella. *"For example, we are strong in mobility, health IT, and security and all three of those areas are in harmony and work to build the industry."*

Georgia's overall economic picture is much improved since the Great Recession of 2008, when job losses exceeded 160,000 and the unemployment rate doubled. It has rebounded nicely with experts noting that the city has emerged stronger and more diversified. Dennis Lockhart, president and CEO of the Federal Reserve Bank of Atlanta, wrote in *The Atlanta Journal Constitution* in September 2015 that the metro economy's recovery is *"well established and better balanced than before the recession."* He noted that the business services sector is showing gains. The area remains a major logistics and transportation hub—*"the improving national economy is boosting those sectors."*

The following table shows average hourly wages for selected occupations in Atlanta compared with the U.S. overall:

Occupation	Atlanta area	United States
Total, in all occupations	$23.44	$22.71
Financial managers	$64.95	$62.61
General and operations managers	$58.17	$56.35
Management analysts	$44.92	$43.68
Computer systems analysts	$39.53	$41.98
Accountants and auditors	$37.98	$35.42
Registered nurses	$31.27	$35.55
Customer service representatives	$17.39	$16.29
Construction laborers	$13.38	$17.19
Retail salespersons	$12.20	$12.38
Cashiers	$9.33	$9.93
Waiters and waitresses	$9.20	$10.40
Cooks, fast food	$8.80	$9.15

Source: U.S. Bureau of Labor Statistics Occupational Employment Statistics May 2014.

State Farm is a strong example of Atlanta's draw for technology hiring. Atlanta is a major employment hub for State Farm, with 6,000 employees in the metro area. State Farm plans to hire another 3,000 as it builds out a 2.2-million-square-foot development at Perimeter Center in Dunwoody.

Business-friendly Beyond Downtown

Some of Georgia's biggest cities—Atlanta, Columbus, Augusta and Savannah—have the largest number of businesses in the state, but the most profitable businesses are in the suburbs and smaller cities. Six places in the top 10, each with a population under 60,000, boast higher average revenue per business than the state's most populous cities.

According to NerdWallet, the best places in suburban metro Atlanta to start a business are:

1. Alpharetta – With almost 60,000 residents, Alpharetta is the largest city in the top 10. It has nearly 9,000 businesses, which average over $6.9 million in revenue per business each year, more than any city on this list.

2. Doraville – Doraville's average revenue per business ($5,361,780) is second only to Alpharetta. The city's proximity to Atlanta, major transportation routes and two of the state's largest airports make it a prime location for businesses.

3. Vinings – Home to over 1,700 businesses, Vinings is in a favorable location between two major interstates and ten minutes from downtown Atlanta.

4. Cumming – Cumming is one of the smallest cities on this list, but it has more business per 100 people than anyplace in this study. In fact, Cumming has almost as many businesses (5,251) as it does residents (5,504).

5. Norcross – Entrepreneurs eyeing Norcross for their business ventures can take advantage of free mentoring and workshops through Score Atlanta, a nonprofit resource center for small businesses. Business incentives in the state-designated opportunity zone, such as a $3,500 per job tax credit, are also a bonus for business owners. These perks may contribute to the high concentration of businesses in Norcross.

A Meeting Destination

Atlanta also is a major destination for meetings and conferences, with the World Congress Center Authority ranking among the top five largest convention destinations in the country. In 2015, Atlanta hosted eighteen major citywide conventions and over the next three years is already confirmed to host fifty more.

In 2014, hotel occupancy levels in the city rose over 70 percent for the first time in Atlanta's history. Growth in hotel occupancy across the metro area was up 8.1 percent year-over-year, ranking Atlanta No. 1 among the top 25 destinations in the U.S.

CHAPTER 12

PRACTICAL NOTEBOOK ON MOVING

Credit: Peachtree Movers

Moving to Atlanta, like to most major metropolitan areas, requires careful planning. According to Julie Hughes, owner of Peachtree Movers, a 40-year-old Atlanta-based moving company focused on local intown moves, it's important to book early, especially in the busy months between May and August when people tend to move because their children are out of school for the summer break. Atlanta's temperate weather makes moving a 365-days-a-year activity, with only an ice storm affecting a move, according to local moving experts.

Atlanta's Busiest Moving Season

"During our busy season, we are booked seven days a week. You wouldn't be able to get a move scheduled even a month out, " said Hughes, suggesting that people reserve a mover a minimum of six weeks out.

Even during the Great Recession, her business continued to grow for residential moves, though corporate relocations came to a standstill. *"No matter what people were still moving to Atlanta. The interest rates were cheaper. "*

She recommends that people move on a Sunday, Monday or Tuesday since those days tend to book up last and often times a moving company will offer a discount to move on those days.

Unpredictability of Atlanta Traffic Patterns

Another important factor in moving to the Peach State's largest city is the realities of traffic, with rush hour often starting as early as 3:30 in some parts of the metro area. Hughes said because the traffic in Atlanta is so unpredictable, moving firms will use GPS to avoid some of the worst congestion. Customers should ask if a mover will work with them if there is stopped traffic for prolonged periods of time.

How do people ensure that their mover is reputable? When it comes to local movers, Hughes said find out how long a company has been in business—that will determine if it's well established. *"Go to BBB and check if they have any open claims. Make sure they have an A+ rating."* Hughes observed that online reviews are not always a good indication of reputable providers, since there are ways to push bad reviews further out on search engine results.

Here are some of the more established local movers in metro Atlanta:

- All My Sons
- Atlanta Peach Movers
- Bulldog Movers (also Buckhead Movers)
- Mark the Mover
- Peachtree Movers
- Two Men & A Truck

Intown Moves to High-Rises Take Longer

Many intown moves for younger people in Atlanta involve going into a high-rise apartment or condo, which could add more time than what a person might think. *"If you are moving downtown or to Midtown in a high rise, it's a lot more complicated,"* Hughes said. It requires reserving an elevator, and letting a landlord know that the moving crew will be in the building. *"It takes longer to move from a two-bedroom house to a two-bedroom apartment on the thirty-eighth floor because you have elevators involved."*

Movers tend to hit more traffic if they are moving someone intown versus to the suburbs, she added.

Go to *Moving to Atlanta's* website for a four-week checklist of things to do heading to the move day.

CHAPTER 13

IMPORTANT PHONE NUMBERS AND RESOURCE LINKS

GO ONLINE FOR OUR EXTENSIVE LIST OF ATLANTA AREA RESOURCES

For the latest information about moving to and living in the Atlanta area, please visit our companion website:

www.MovingtoAtlantaGuide.com.

If you need to access our extensive resource pages quickly, go directly to: www.MovingtoAtlantaGuide.com/resources.

Important Phone Numbers and Website Links

State Information and Services

Drivers Licenses
www.dds.ga.gov
404-657-9300

Fishing or Hunting Licenses
www.georgiawildlife.com
800-366-2661

Voter Registration
www.sos.ga.gov
404-656-2881

Utilities

Electricity
www.georgiaemc.com/emcs-of-georgia/search-by-county

Natural Gas
www.psc.state.ga.us/gas/certified_marketers.asp

Cable/Satellite/Phone/Internet

DIRECTV
www.directv.com

Comcast Xfinity
www.xfinity.com

AT&T U-Verse
www.att.com

Charter Spectrum
www.charter.com

Note: *For water, sewer & garbage collection services, see county websites.*

Transportation

Bus Services
www.atltransit.org

Uber
www.uber.com/cities/atlanta

Hospitals

Wellstar Health System
www.wellstar.org

Emory Healthcare
www.emoryhealthcare.org

Grady Health System
www.gradyhealth.org

Northside Hospital
www.northside.com

Piedmont Healthcare
www.piedmont.org

Dekalb Medical
www.dekalbmedical.org

Gwinnett Medical Center
www.gwinnettmedicalcenter.org

County Information, Services, and Schools

Note: *This list does not include Atlanta Public School, City Schools of Decatur, or Marietta City Schools.*

Clayton County
www.claytoncountyga.gov

Clayton County Schools
www.clayton.k12.ga.us
770-473-2700

Cobb County
www.cobbcounty.org

Cobb County School District
www.cobbk12.org
770-426-3300

DeKalb County
www.dekalbcountyga.gov
404-371-2000

DeKalb County Schools
www.dekalb.k12.ga.us
678-676-1200

Douglas County
www.celebratedouglascounty.com
770.949.2000

Douglas County Schools
www.douglas.k12.ga.us
770-651-2000

Fayette County
www.fayettecountyga.gov

Fayette County Public Schools
www.fcboe.org
770-460-3535

Fulton County
www.fultoncountyga.gov
404-612-4000

Fulton County Schools
www.fultonschools.org
470-254-3600

Gwinnett County
www.gwinnettcounty.com
770-822-8000

Gwinnett County Public Schools
www.gwinnett.k12.ga.us
678-301-6000

Henry County
www.co.henry.ga.us

Henry County Schools
770-957-6601
www.henry.k12.ga.us

City Information, Services and Schools

Alpharetta
www.alpharetta.ga.us
678-297-6000

Atlanta
www.atlantaga.gov

Atlanta Public Schools
www.atlantapublicschools.us
(404) 802-3500

Avondale Estates
www.avondaleestates.org
404-294-5400

Brookhaven
www.brookhavenga.gov

Chamblee
www.chambleega.com
770-986-5010

Clarkston
www.clarkstonga.gov

College Park
www.collegeparkga.com
404-767-1537

Decatur
www.decaturga.com
404-370-4100

City Schools of Decatur
www.csdecatur.net
404-371-3601

Dunwoody
www.dunwoodyga.gov
678-382-6700

East Point
www.eastpointcity.org

Hapeville
www.hapeville.org
404-669-2100

Marietta
www.mariettaga.gov

Marietta City Schools
www.marietta-city.org
770-422-3500

Norcross
www.norcrossga.net
770-448-2122

Peachtree City
www.peachtree-city.org
770-487-7657

Sandy Springs
www.sandyspringsga.org

Roswell
www.roswellgov.com
770-641-3727

CONCLUSION

Singer-songwriter John Mayer once said, *"Atlanta's my musical home. It really was the place where I really came alive."*

That sums up the feeling for many who have chosen to live and work in this unique city of neighborhoods and urban energy, with its blend of new and old traditions, natural beauty, and welcoming Southern charm.

Without question, people moving to Atlanta need to be strategic about where they live and where they work—the realities of Atlanta traffic and a rapidly growing population demand it. The good news is there are many choices for both, and enough places to unwind and relax that a person will never get bored. Atlanta's neighborhoods are strong and growing, with unlimited things to do. There's an opportunity to connect and build a future, regardless of a person's age or stage of life. And, with the advent of the Atlanta Beltline, amazing things are happening in neighborhoods all over the city, as a new focus on walkability and greenspaces takes hold.

What a great time to be part of Atlanta's story—from the technology corridors of Midtown and Alpharetta, to the movie-making magic building in Atlanta and beyond—the city is vibrating with energy. It's *alive*.

For those who call Atlanta home, this is a chance to have a voice in redefining what this place will be for future generations. One thing is clear: Lots of people want to be part of that future.

We hope you see yourself here, too.

ACKNOWLEDGEMENTS

I am thankful to many people for helping me capture the spirit of Atlanta in this book. Beginning with my family, I want to thank my husband, Jeff, who has been incredibly supportive of my book research and writing for this current book and my earlier book projects, and my two children, who are my biggest supporters and who accompanied me on many photo shoots around the city. I also appreciate my brother-in-law Jonathan Sargent, who shared his diverse network of contacts in several of Atlanta's intown areas.

Below are a few special individuals who went above and beyond in helping me tell the Atlanta story: Dante Stephensen, an inspiring Atlanta visionary and restauranteur who fell in love with this city nearly five decades ago; Carrie Burns, founder of Atlanta Movie Tours and the president of the Castleberry Hill Homeowners Association, who shared her insights on Atlanta's art scene and burgeoning film industry, and who graciously hosted my book launch party at her film tourism shop; Bill de St. Aubin, CEO of Sizemore Group, whose decades-long efforts to help make Atlanta communities more walkable and livable are an amazing legacy to us all; Linda Mattingly with Hometura Realty, and Melissa Miller and Pat Westrick of The Pat & Melissa Group, Re/Max Metro Atlanta Cityside, for their insights on Atlanta's real estate market; and Rob Caiello, vice president of Marketing for Allconnect, for simplifying the complex landscape of utility services in the metro area. Also, a very special thank you to Jordan and Erin Wakefield and their amazing team at The Smoke Ring for catering my book launch party and Amy MacKinnon for her photography talents. Thanks also to Mari Ann Stefanelli Perusek, an amazing editor and knowledgeable resource on all things "in the ATL."

While I'm indebted to all the individuals who were interviewed in this book, I want to call out these individuals—author and urban visionary Ryan Gravel; Michael Crandal with the Buckhead Business Coalition; Tino Mantella, CEO of the Technology Association of Georgia; Dennis Mobley, president of the Inman Park Neighborhood Association; Debbie Hughes, owner of Peachtree Movers; Debbie Michaud, editor of *Creative Loafing Atlanta*, and Eric Champlin, editor and founder of *Atlanta Trails.com*, for your contributions to key chapters. Also thanks to Brian Carr, director of Marketing and Communications for Midtown Alliance; Pam Ledbetter, president, Accent Creative Group; Linda Coatsworth, for her award-winning nature photograph of Atlanta's fall splendor; and Matthew Dotson, economist with the Southeast Information Office of the U.S. Bureau of Labor Statistics.

Finally, to my publisher Newt Barrett with Voyager Media, thanks for the opportunity to be your first book author for the Peach State. It's an honor, and I hope it marks what will be a long-term editorial partnership.

ABOUT THE AUTHOR

A native of Dayton, Ohio, Anne Wainscott-Sargent moved to Atlanta in 1998. She is a writer, blogger and strategic storyteller specializing in the tech, publishing and education sectors. An avid history buff and movie-goer, she loves following Atlanta's growing film industry, connecting with other writers in the Atlanta area, and enjoying the natural beauty of the Chattahoochee River's many bicycle paths. She and her husband live in suburban Atlanta with their two children. She hopes to finish her first novel, a work of historical fiction, in 2016.

Visit Anne's consulting website at: www.annewainscott.com/writing-consulting-services or her blog at: www.annewainscott.com/blog.

Connect with her on Twitter: @annewainscott

Printed in Great Britain
by Amazon